CW00551917

DRUG
SMUGGLING

A source is the person in the country of origin who gets the load together to be smuggled into the Unite Finding a source brings up one of the most pressing eth tions that comes into play in the drug-smuggling game.

CHAPTER 3

FINDING A SOURCE

If a smuggler has met a source on his own, then there is no problem. Problems arise when a person has met a source through someone else in the drug business. When this happens, the ethical thing to do is to get permission to use the source or to pay for the privilege. A good source man is probably the most valuable member of the smuggling team; consequently, people are rarely enthusiastic about learning that their source has taken on another customer.

The $11-billion U.S. drug-fighting budget is the biggest factor that has changed the hunt for a drug source. Paid informants, snitches, rollovers—the number of these people has vastly increased, and they're lurking in the bars of Miami and on the docks of New York. When they gain the trust of a developing smuggling group, it makes whatever agency is paying them very happy.

If you are branching off from another smuggling group and want to use the same source, you are not going to be able to do it behind the first group's back. These things always come out, and then you look like a sneak trying to steal the contact. The best way is to pay the smuggler who originally found the contact. If he refuses to deal, then get out and find a contact of your own. Source people are out there, and they want to do business as much as you do. Neither party can advertise for business contacts, but by knowing where to look, a potential smuggler can find the link he needs to provide the cargo and foreign-country support systems he needs to smuggle. Here are the rules to follow:

Rule 1: Don't search for this golden person in the United States. The United States may be fighting a war on drugs, but no matter what you hear or read, Mexico, Colombia, and Jamaica are just lip-service allies in that war. You have to go to these countries to find a source.

Mexico and Jamaica are easy. They have huge American tourist industries, and all shapes, sizes, and colors of Americans come and go, needing only proof of American citizenship. Colombia is a different story. Years of bad publicity about cartels and kidnapping have scared off most Americans. For your initial trip, it's best to go as part of a tour group visiting ruins. If you don't, you'll get shaken down by everyone from the Colombian entry customs guy to the police in the street, wondering what you're doing there. Find a tour that is going to the area you are interested in — Santa Marta or Barranquilla. In Mexico, a good starting spot is Chihuahua; in Jamaica, Montego Bay or Negril.

My smuggling partner Bart liked to do what he called "the world tour." We'd rent a single-engine airplane and fly from Florida to the Bahamas, then move down the island chains and hit Haiti and Jamaica, then Mexico. We'd stop at a different place every night and just meet people and see what developed. More often than not, people we met would bring up the drug subject and then we'd just listen to what they had to say.

Rule 2: Check into the nicest hotel, slip the bartender a $100 bill, and indicate to him that you'd like to meet someone who can supply marijuana or cocaine in substantial weights. This will start the ball rolling. Every big hotel or resort has a person to handle the unusual needs of the guests, and the word of what your needs are will get to the right person.

If nothing happens fast enough, just walking down the streets will bring out teenagers offering to sell you dope and girls. Give them a word of encouragement, and they'll be off to find their cousin, who is a big dealer and knows where to get big weight. More often than not, these kids will take the few dollars you give them and disappear, but if things aren't happening yet you don't have a whole lot to lose in seeing if they bring anyone back for a meeting.

Rule 3: Go directly to the police or customs people. Yes, in the United States, law-enforcement personnel are generally well paid and can't be bribed. This is definitely not the case in drug-source countries. In these countries, the police and other law enforcement agencies are on the side of the drug trade. All you have to do is pay them to get their cooperation.

The police don't want to deal directly with an American, but they will certainly know a person to put you in contact with who can handle your needs and wants. The police to contact are ones in small towns. Don't walk into the Montego Bay police station, but go to the other side of the island to Sav-la-Mar, slip a low-ranking cop $100 (which will be two weeks pay for him), and tell him what you are looking for. To an American mind used to dealing with American police, this probably sounds incredibly foolish, but it works.

Once you've been introduced to your source man, you have to decide whether he is capable of taking care of what needs to be done. Shit-talkers exist everywhere. A source man is going to have your life in his hands at one time or another, and you want to be confident that he can do the job so those thoughts of spending ten years in a Colombian jail are kept to a minimum.

The three major areas a drug source man is responsible for are as follows: 1) finding the load and getting it together for shipping; 2) finding the landing strip or dock that is going to be used for the loading and making sure all fuel and equipment are at the scene; and 3) paying off everyone who needs to be paid off. That's why your source man is so important—he basically is in charge of the whole operation in the drug-producing country. All the smuggler does is show up.

Understand that a source person has accumulated a lot of experience or has a lot of political backing to have reached his position.

You're a greenhorn in the drug business, and no matter what you think your credentials are, you aren't going to roll into town and tell him how to do his end of the deal. That is the first step in developing the trust that has to exist with the source person.

Once you start talking, make sure you understand everything that is being said. Source people who have dealt with Americans over the years can usually speak passable English. But if you're not understanding what your source man is saying and you don't speak Spanish, find someone who can translate. Don't be embarrassed to ask for clarifications to make sure everyone knows what is being talked about.

Don't be in a big hurry to leave. It is not financially or logistically practical to run back to Santa Marta, Colombia, every time your source man wants to go over a new coordinate where you'll meet the mother ship or show you a new airstrip he wants to use because the one you thought you were going to use has been blown up. The adventure of visiting the source country will wear off quickly. It's time wasted on travel, with living expenses, and you don't want to get too well known by the customs people and locals.

Smugglers always want assurance from their source man that they are going to be getting the highest-quality goods. The answer is always "great stuff, the best." That area brought up, it is then best to leave it at that. Here's why:

The drug business operates on a fronted-goods market. A small amount of money is paid up front, but everyone does not get paid in full till the money flows back down from the ultimate user. That means that everyone involved has a stake in the success of the mission.

The next thing you'll talk about with your source is the price. Let's say we are dealing with Jamaican marijuana. You agree on a price of $150 a pound for a five-hundred-pound load. That's $75,000 to the source man. But you aren't going to, nor are you expected to, pay all of that up front. With new customers, a source man is going to want 25 to 30 percent up front, but for older customers this could drop to as little as 10 percent.

Once the source man has this up-front money, he goes to his grower contacts and buys what they have. The growers rarely

Smuggler: Is the stuff going to be good?

Source Man: Primo, the best.

Smuggler: How about the landing strip? In good condition with no holes or soft spots?

CHAPTER 4

TRUST ME, SEÑOR

Source Man: Yes, very good condition. I was out there yesterday. It's ready to receive you.

Smuggler: Good. How about the fuel? You've got a thousand gallons of aviation fuel and the pumps?

Source Man: No problem, it will be there waiting for you. I pay and the police get it and bring it out.

Smuggler: How about the payoffs? The airstrip owners, the police, the army? Everyone taken care of?

Source Man: Relax, amigo. This is my job. Everyone's paid.

Smuggler: We're coming at 9 A.M. your time. You'll have that hand-held radio set on 122.2, right?

Source Man: 9 A.M., me and my men will be there at sunup. We'll turn the radio on at 8 A.M. and wait for your call. Everything is all set. Come on down and we'll make lots of money.

J.S., our American source man living in Colombia, and his Colombian partner, Julio, were fronting the goods for a DC-3 trip Gene and I were going to make to Colombia. The above conversation took place two days before our launch. This is what actually happened.

When Gene and I arrived over the coast of Colombia, right on time, haze and smoke limited our visibility to two miles. Gene had used this strip once before, so we dropped down to five hundred feet and navigated using time and distance calculations to get in the vicinity of the landing strip, which was nothing more than a dirt road. Then we could call on the radio and notify the ground crew so they could light some tires on fire or vector us in from the sound of our engines.

I made the radio call when we determined we were within five miles of the strip. No answer. There were no navigation aids, we could barely see a mile in front of us, and we were looking for a stretch of road with a clump of trees at one end and a rickety barn to the west of where we should touch down to avoid potholes.

After twenty minutes, Gene found what he thought was the strip. We didn't have any choice but to come in and land; we were almost out of fuel. Still no answer on the radio.

We touched down and taxied to a stop. Gene was sure this was the place. No one was around. We walked over to the clump of trees to take a leak, and sitting against a tree was a dark-skinned Colombian. Next to him was a radio with the batteries lying in disarray next to it.

The Colombian didn't know anything except that we were to wait. Thirty minutes later, Julio came riding up on a horse and told us how happy he was to see us, and that J.S. should be there any minute.

Julio left and came back half an hour later with twenty fifty-five-gallon drums of fuel on a flatbed truck. But there were no pumps to transfer the fuel. We started dumping the fuel into our five-gallon can and then walked up on the wing and dumped it into the fuel tanks. Two hours later, still no J.S. By this time, every villager who had heard the airplane land had come out to the scene wanting a job fueling the plane or providing lunch.

After three hours, a single-engine Piper swooped low over the strip and we could see J.S.'s smiling face as he waved at us. But the plane didn't land. It continued to another airstrip to land, which added another half hour before J.S.'s actual arrival on the scene in a police jeep.

We had then been on the ground four hours, and J.S. announced that the marijuana wasn't there but a hundred miles away at a landing strip on the Guajira Peninsula. A Colombian version of the FBI was with J.S., along with an army officer. These three, plus Julio, Gene, and I, got in the DC-3 and flew the forty-five minutes back to the Caribbean coast.

The Guajira has hundreds of landing strips dotting the landscape, and I could see that the FBI-type guy, who was supposed to know the location of the strip, was having trouble figuring out which one had the cargo waiting for us. We circled for half an hour, and no one showed themselves on the ground. Finally, we gave up and flew back to the original landing strip.

No sooner were we out of the DC-3 than brown-uniformed soldiers were aiming weapons at us. Julio, hearing bullets zipping over our heads, yelled to run. We leaped into a nearby ditch. When the soldiers got to the airplane they stopped shooting, and Julio and the two government officials went to talk things over.

We were motioned out of the ditch, and Gene, J.S., and I were encircled by soldiers and told to sit down.

Haggling between Julio and the soldiers went on for a few minutes, then a big wad of Colombian money changed hands, and we were told we were free to go.

Julio said that maybe all the Americans had better leave; there had been some mix-up with the payoffs to the army. So J.S., Gene, and I cranked up the DC-3 and flew away empty-handed, back to the United States.

As soon as the landing gear was retracted, J.S. immediately started telling us how none of the fuck-ups were his fault. Gene and I looked at each other, thinking the same thing—that we should throw J.S. into the Caribbean. Of all the things J.S. had assured us were taken care of, only the fuel was on scene. Three months of work, and tens of thousands of our dollars, were down the drain.

A conspiracy is defined as "an agreement between two or more people to commit a crime." From the minute a group is assembled for the purpose of drug smuggling, the conspiracy to smuggle drugs has begun, and there should be a firm "need to know" covenant in

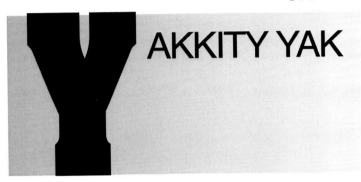

CHAPTER 5

YAKKITY YAK

place which makes it clear that no one talks to anyone else about drug smuggling unless that person is part of the group.

The biggest problem with communication involves the telephone. A telephone is something everyone grew up with, but the sooner you look at it as the enemy the better off you are.

The problems with telephones take three main forms: 1) wiretaps, 2) "pen" taps, and 3) the records generated. If someone is busted, one of the first things law enforcement will do is subpoena that person's telephone records.

So the telephone is your enemy, but one you can't do business without. Of course, the best way to defeat phone paranoia would be not to have a phone at home, but that isn't practical. Therefore, the rules are as follows:

▶ *Never talk smuggling-related topics on your home phone.* This is especially important if you have a cordless phone, because cordless radio transmissions can be picked up by anyone in the local area. You might think you're clever using the term "tomatoes" instead of marijuana, but you're not. If someone is listening, the sentence "I think the second week in April is a good time to go on vacation to the beach and buy two hundred pounds of shrimp" is not going to fool anyone.

▶ *Don't make a long-distance call from your home to anyone you are working with.* So what can you do with your home telephone? The only way a home telephone can be of use is for a fellow conspirator to let you know that he needs to talk. Each group member should find three pay telephones near his house and label them #1, #2, and #3. This information should be exchanged among the group members. Then if someone wants to talk to another group member, all he has to do is call that person from a pay phone and tell him to go out to his #2 for a call at forty-five past the hour.

In choosing these pay phones, stay away from places that are busy and where it would look odd to be hanging around waiting to receive a call. Phone banks outside libraries or convenience stores are good spots, especially if you can find two phones together, since a caller can call the other one if the first one he tries is busy. Also, make sure the pay phone can receive incoming calls.

In reality, court-authorized wiretaps are very rare. *Newsweek* reports that in 1990 there were 872 state and federal court-approved wiretaps in the United States. A court-ordered wiretap is an expensive proposition for the government because of the manpower it sucks up. I can't say that a wiretap would never be used against an entrepreneurial smuggling operation, but it would be rare.

"Pen" taps also have to be court-authorized, but they don't require the extensive manpower involved in listening to all of the recorded material. A pen tap detects and records all phone calls to and from a specific telephone. These pen taps aren't worth much as evidence, but they are helpful in enlarging an investigation.

Then there are the "records." Today, I see a device that can give the authorities a record of almost every phone call I make from my home phone. Pay cash for your calls by using a pay phone so there is no billing record that can come back to haunt you. This means having rolls of quarters close by, but that's just part of the price of doing business.

For communications of a less immediate nature, an answering service will work. These services most likely will want you to appear in person to begin, but a few might let you handle the whole thing on the telephone. You obviously don't want to use your real name; if asked for identification, you can always say you forgot your wallet and go try another place.

Once you have an answering service, it allows other group members to leave messages for you, as well as providing your source man with a contact point to call. It is also a perfect spot for packages and COD orders to be sent.

Another form of message service available involves the use of a toll-free 800 number. This costs two to three times more than a local answering service, but if your group is scattered about the country, the extra expense might be worth it.

Communication with the source man should be kept to an absolute minimum. Phone service in source countries is not near the level it is in the United States, and pay phones are almost nonexistent. This means that the source man has to have a telephone where you can reach him. In Colombia, Eduardo had a business where we could call him during the daylight hours. However, when working with Rasta Nigel in Jamaica I had to call his cousin's house and leave word that I would call the next day at a certain time to talk to him. If either of these people wanted to initiate the communication, they had the number of my answering service.

Respecting the telephone for the amount of damage and paranoia it can inflict as a result of misuse is of utmost importance. I compare telephone mistakes to speeding. If you speed all the time, it is inevitable that you are going to get some speeding tickets. But if you make a conscious effort not to speed, then the few times you must, you'll have the odds in your favor.

Other communication situations that can present problems include the following:

▶ *Bars and restaurants.* Someone has a few too many drinks and raises his voice, and a passing waiter or a diner at the next table overhears.

▶ *Airport ramps or boat marinas.* Police units in south Florida stake themselves out using parabolic microphones that can pick up conversations from two hundred yards away.

So remember, use only pay phones, don't talk in public places, and confine conversations to private homes and cars, and you'll be 99-percent worry-free when it comes to compromising your mission to unwanted listeners. If you have a group member who doesn't see the value in these communication rules, he should be terminated from the team.

Being asked to show identification is a possibility in so many facets of the drug-smuggling business that every participant should have a credible set of fake IDs that he can use to conceal his true identity.

CHAPTER 6

FAKE IDENTIFICATION

Possessing fake ID is at most a misdemeanor crime, but as long as it isn't used in conjunction with a defrauding scheme, it is rare for anything other than confiscation to result if you're caught with it.

Fake IDs are a big business in the United States, needed by everyone from underage drinkers to illegal aliens. There are two ways to procure a set of fake IDs—buying one outright or building your own. Building your own is not hard; it just takes a little planning.

The following are are some excellent ways to get a set of fake ID:

▶ *Buy it on the Mexican-American border.* A few hundred dollars will buy a driver's license with photo, a Social Security card, and a birth certificate. From that you can immediately present yourself as someone else. The section of Tijuana, Nogales, or any Mexican border town where the strip joints and bars are is where you'll find the hustlers to steer you to the ID makers.

▶ *Get a friend to give you his IDs.* Then he can report his wallet lost and have all of them reissued. The problem with this is if something bizarre happens and any kind of police pressure is applied to your friend, he is going to tell the truth. You may not want to put a friend on the spot like this—not only do you tip him off that you're up to something, but when the shit starts rolling you'll have an innocent person caught in the conspiracy.

▶ *Get a U.S. passport in a phony name.* This is the best fake ID of all, but getting one takes time and planning. This is definitely illegal, and the risk involved can be justified only if you are confronted with the fugitive option. Leaving or entering the country using a false passport is stupid unless you are a wanted man. Frederick Forsyth wrote a few nice pages in *The Day of the Jackal* about how one of his characters got perfect fake IDs, including a British passport. Unfortunately, accomplishing what the Jackal did is a bit harder these days, although it certainly can still be done.

To start, acquire the driver's license of a person of the opposite sex. Bribe an ID checker at a college bar, so when he confiscates a fake ID he'll pass it on to you. Then rent a P.O. box or a dirt-cheap room with its own address. Once you have these, the paperwork begins.

If you happen to know of a friend or relative who died young, you're ahead of the game. You want someone who would be about the same age as you are. If you know the date and place of death, then you can get a death certificate. A death certificate is public record, and it contains a person's full name, place of birth, date of birth, and mother's maiden name (and Social Security number, if the person had one).

Call the county records bureau in the county where the person died to find out what is required. Most will charge a small fee of about $5, ask that you state your relationship to the dead person, and require you to enclose a photocopy of your driver's license. Copy the driver's license confiscated from the female and enclose a money order requesting that the death certificate be sent to your new mailing address.

With the information from the death certificate in hand, you can then proceed to get a birth certificate. Again, call the county records office and ask what the requirements are for a replacement birth certificate. Most likely you will just have to send a letter stating that you need your birth certificate, plus a money order to cover costs. Change the name on the mail-drop address to coincide with the name of the person whose identity you are assuming, and wait for your birth certificate to arrive. Make sure you ask for a legal birth certificate with a raised seal on it, not just a photocopy of a hospital record.

(If you would rather assume the identity of someone you have never known, go to the library and get back copies of the local newspaper. Look through the obituaries until you find someone who died who was close to your age and who had a detailed obituary written about him. If the obit gives you enough information, you can go right to obtaining a birth certificate. If not, then get the death certificate first.)

The birth certificate is the key. Once you have this document you are on your way to getting an amazing set of IDs. If you have knowledge of a Social Security number, you can write for a replacement card. You can register to vote and receive a voter's card. With a Social Security card in hand you can even open up a checking account. Get a library card and have some business cards printed up using your fake name and address. The possibilities for these nonphoto IDs are numerous. Call first to find out what the requirements are, then get all you can.

The first picture ID to get is a proof-of-age card that all states issue to people who don't drive. New York is a great place for one of these since so many people in New York City don't drive. With a proof-of-age picture ID, it's easy to go right to a driver's license. Visit a large city, get a mail-drop address, and head for the driver's license bureau.

For a driver's license, you generally need three kinds of identification. A call ahead will ensure that you are ready with the required ID and, assuming you pass the driving test, you'll have a license to drive.

With a birth certificate, a Social Security card, a proof-of-age card from one state, a driver's license from another state, plus assorted fill-in IDs, you now have a great set of fake IDs. If you want to go for a passport, you'll have no problem.

This may all sound like a lot of work and expense — changing cities, getting different mail-drop addresses, and so on. It is, but the object is to get a set of IDs that will not link you in any way to your real identity.

It is all part of the process to have to listen to people propose to buy a World War II surplus submarine or a thirty-year-old Boeing 707 four-engine jet for a smuggling mission. But after the fantasy trips are bullshitted about, then the reality will evolve about what equipment you will need to accomplish the mission.

CHAPTER 7

SHOPPING

An equipment list is easily broken down to aircraft, boats, cars and trucks, and accessories or gadgets.

The first rule to understand is that most equipment, more than likely, is not going to live very long. Seizure, abandonment, and crashes will gobble up equipment, and few items will ever be resold or traded in. This rule is important, because it dictates how much money to spend for a piece of equipment, as well as how to register it once you purchase it.

No matter how expensive a piece of equipment is or how attached you might be to it, remember that you only need it to accomplish the mission. If the mission is a success and the equipment can be used again, you're lucky. If the mission fails and the equipment is lost, it can be replaced.

When you buy a boat, airplane, truck or car, it's best to buy it from a private party. By private party, I mean an individual who owns the equipment, not a company or dealership. Individuals selling equipment are anxious to sell.

If you want to pay with green money, remember IRS Form 4789 regarding transactions involving more than $10,000 in cash. This form does not apply to a private-party transaction as it does to a transaction between businesses. However, when you offer to pay cash, the seller's instinct will be that it's drug money. If a seller doesn't want to accept cash, try someone else. A high percentage of people in a position to own airplanes and boats have their own tricks to play, and a cash sale opens up lots of tricking possibilities with the tax man.

It's nice to accomplish the transaction on a Saturday or Sunday when banks are closed. Have a ballpark figure worked out with the seller and have fake identification ready. If the seller wants to wait until Monday to transact the deal at his bank, and the bank wants you to fill out IRS Form 4789, don't.

It used to be easy to walk into a bank and buy a cashier's check if you didn't want to pay in cash. The $10,000 cash transaction rule still applied, but you could just buy $9,000 in cashier's checks until you had your sum. However, banks are now much more strict regarding whom they will sell cashier's checks to — usually it includes only people with an account at that bank. Let your fingers do the walking — if you're interested in cashier's checks, call ahead to determine bank policy.

Another possibility is to open a bogus checking account. Once you have that established, it's easy to go by the drive-up window every day and make a cash deposit (keep it under $10,000) till you have the account balance built up to where you want it, then you can either write a personal check for the equipment or have the bank issue a cashier's check from funds in the account.

Note: A bogus checking account should only be used for a short period of time and never for more than three purchases. If something goes wrong, law enforcement can seize the assets of the account. Also, having a lot of money in a bank with a fake ID and a signature card being the only link between you and it can be downright nerve-racking.

Always exhaust private-party possibilities before you go to a broker or dealership, especially when buying a boat or an airplane. It is common for professional sellers to happily accept your money and then call the DEA or customs to report the transaction.

Airplanes

The mechanics of airborne smuggling are dangerous. The main reason involves takeoff after the cargo is loaded. Pilots contemplating drug-smuggling trips must have at least an instrument rating, understand how to use the handbooks and charts available to figure out how much runway a plane needs to get airborne when it is 20 percent over gross takeoff weight, and have enough mechanical knowledge to understand how an aircraft fuel system works. An airborne smuggling checklist is long, and every item is important. Don't get involved in airborne smuggling if you're not already an accomplished pilot.

I learned early on that airplanes will still fly when they are over their maximum gross weight. In Vietnam we would cram as many people and as much cargo into an 0-2 airplane as would fit. As long as there was enough runway, the plane would get airborne with loads in the area of 20 to 30 percent over gross weight.

But you don't fly by the seat of your pants in the drug business. Know how much over gross weight your airplane is going to be when loaded and how much runway will be needed. Remember to add extra length for rough field conditions and a no-wind or tail-wind component. Both *Aircraft Price Digest* and *Business Aircraft* publish literature that makes it easy to compare the important capabilities of the various makes of aircraft.

Have a prepurchase inspection done on the aircraft. This costs $50 to $100, and includes a check of the logbooks to verify that all inspections are in order, as well as a cylinder compression check.

Get at least an hour of flying time on the aircraft before you buy it, even if you have to pay the owner for the time. Make sure all the radio equipment works and check the oil consumption of the engine. Acceptable oil consumption can go from one quart every fifteen hours of flight to half a quart every hour. Why some engines use more oil than others is hard to figure out, but you definitely don't want one that likes to suck oil.

Do a title search on the airplane. The Federal Aviation Administration (FAA) keeps records on all aircraft registered in the United States. By doing a title search you'll be able to confirm that the person who is selling you the aircraft is the actual owner, as well as confirming that there are no liens filed against the ownership of the aircraft. If the seller can't clear up any lien problems that exist before you buy the aircraft, don't buy. There are several companies based in Oklahoma City that do title searches, and you can also find a listing of title search companies in *Trade-A-Plane*. A title search costs in the area of $40.

When you purchase an airplane, the only document you need is an FAA bill-of-sale form signed by the seller in ink. You don't have to fill out the "buyer" section in advance, just the seller section, so it is very possible that you can get the signed bill of sale without the seller ever knowing what name or company you are going to register the plane under.

It is possible — and it often happens — that a new buyer will never bother to reregister the plane. As far as the FAA knows, the plane was never sold. This isn't a good idea. The FAA makes it so easy to register airplanes that there is no reason not to do it.

There is a possibility that FAA legislation will be passed that would require a person registering an aircraft to do so in person and present picture identification to prove his identity. If this happens in 1992 or 1993, it will just be another excellent reason to make sure you have excellent fake ID and a mail-drop address.

An autopilot is essential for an airborne drug-smuggling mission. Flights are long, and a round-trip flight from the United States to Colombia and back can mean twenty-four to forty hours of nonstop flying. This is a long time for one guy to have to keep his hands on the controls. Plus, unlike copilots, autopilots don't weigh two hundred pounds or require a lawyer and bail money if the mission is busted.

Installing an autopilot yourself is expensive, and a certain amount of flight time is required to work out the bugs. There are plenty of airplanes out there with the autopilot already installed.

Very few airplanes can accomplish the well-traveled smuggling routes (Colombia-United States, Jamaica-United States, southern Mexico-United States) without being modified with extra fuel tanks. You can find airplanes with FAA-approved modifications for increased fuel capacity through ads in *Trade-A-Plane* magazine. These ads will also tell you how much fuel capacity can be legally added to the various planes that are approved for modification. However, if you purchase an FAA-approved fuel system modication, don't have it installed at a maintenance shop you aren't well-acquainted with. Often airplanes come out of these shops with "secret" transponders installed. It is far better just to buy the hardware and have a trusted local mechanic install it.

If you end up having to construct your own non-FAA-approved auxiliary fuel system, you have to make it bulletproof and it has to be checked out before the mission begins. I was once flying a Cessna 210 with a rubber-tank gravity-feed system. When I test-flew it, we put 10 gallons into the bladder; when I switched to the auxiliary system the engine immediately died. The bladder tank was designed to hold 150 gallons, but it should have run just fine with 10 gallons remaining in the bladder. Inspection showed that the intake tube in the bladder had curled up rather than staying flat on the bottom of the tank as it was supposed to do. No airplane can accomplish the longer smuggling runs without taking on fuel in the source country. Don't expect an Exxon truck to arrive at your remote jungle strip to fill your plane. Every time I've taken on fuel in a source country it has arrived in 55-gallon drums that look like they've been rusting in a toxic waste dump somewhere. It gets worse when the natives start dumping the fuel into cans, pots, and anything they can get ahold of to pour it into your tanks.

You can't do much about how the fuel is delivered to you, but you can plan ahead so that the fuel that goes into your machine has been filtered properly. Take your own pumps and filtering system down for your first couple of trips.

There are all kinds of pumps available at farm supply or hardware stores, but make sure you invest in one that is approved for gas. Most pumps are for water, and the rubber parts in the pump mechanism will dissolve if gas is being pumped.

Boats

Boats come in all shapes and sizes, as well as prices that can climb to well over a million dollars. Space for the cargo, range of the vessel, ocean-going capabilities, and motor or sail are the criteria used to judge how a boat stacks up. Don't compromise any of these major areas because you think a particular boat would sure be fun to have at your disposal when it's not on a smuggling run.

Like airplanes, boats should be "surveyed" by a professional before they are purchased. The surveyor is looking for problems that the seller might not have told you about or might not know exist. Generally, the cost of a survey is more than made up for by the information you receive. If there is a problem, renegotiate the price with the seller and get the problems fixed.

Once the equipment has been purchased, it should be registered properly before it goes into battle. Correctly registering a boat is important, mainly because of the aggressive position the U.S. Coast Guard has taken involving "safety checks." However, registering any vehicle to be used in a drug-smuggling operation in the name of a real person or real company is a mistake. The coast guard has the right to hail and board any U.S.-registered boat and ask to see the safety equipment aboard. (Of course, this is nothing more than an excuse to check out ownership and registration, plus sniff around for drugs.)

Most big yachts and sailboats have a U.S. registration, while most small boats have a state registration. Check with the state boating authority regarding how to register your boat correctly, or with the coast guard if you have a larger boat. They will tell you exactly what paperwork you have to fill out to make sure you are registered and licensed properly.

Vehicles

Vehicles to haul away the cargo once it is off-loaded are easier to select than boats or airplanes. The appearance of the vehicle comes into play here—new trucks with new camper shells on them are more suspicious than older models that look like they have been around the block a few times.

Three-quarter-ton, eight-foot-bed pickups are the most desirable. The springs and shocks are such that the vehicle won't tilt back if it has a two-thousand-pound load, and these trucks can handle the heaviest camper rigs. Half-ton pickup trucks are far more popular in the marketplace, but unless you beef up the rear suspension, a half-ton pickup will show that it's carrying a heavy load by tilting slightly to the rear.

It is essential that your truck have four-wheel drive. No matter what the mission, you will need a vehicle to off-load to, so have one that is equipped to go anywhere.

Once purchased, if the truck isn't new, then give it the complete razzle-dazzle. The minimum would be four new steel-belted, all-terrain tires and a complete tune-up, including all fluids checked plus new oil and oil filter, plugs, ignition parts, ignition wires, battery, and a radar detector. Additionally, the vehicle should be equipped with a pair of jumper cables, a small tool kit, a flashlight, a road atlas, extra fuses, extra bulbs for the running lights, an extra headlight, a shovel, and a high-lift jack in case you get stuck in sand, mud, or snow.

Each state has different regulations for licensing and registration, but two general rules are to have a legitimate mailing address where you can receive the title and to use "RV" plates as opposed to "business" plates. Recreational vehicle plates on a truck generally exempt you from having to stop at weigh stations. Call the division of motor vehicles in the state in which you are thinking about registering your vehicles to find out the ins and outs of getting the job done. Then you'll know what kind of paperwork to expect when you go in to get your license plates.

There are some other easily purchased items that can be a benefit to the airborne or waterborne smuggler.

Radios

People on the ground need to be able to communicate with folks in the plane (or on the boat). In the last five years there has been a bonanza of reasonably priced hand-held radios that can receive and transmit within a range of forty miles. Twenty miles would be a more accurate number, but for under $400 these radios do the job and have the same 720-channel capability as the ones in an aircraft.

Reliable walkie-talkies and portable cellular phones are available at any Radio Shack store. You can also rent portable cellular phones from the same people who rent you a car. Forget the exotic communications gear like voice scramblers and satellite pagers.

High-frequency (HF) radios can be installed in airplanes or boats and allow radio communications between Colombia and Florida or New York and the Bahamas if atmospheric conditions are good (sunspot flare-ups, if occurring, render HF radios almost useless). Any aircraft or boat radio shop can give you detailed information on HF radios.

Security

Get a catalog from any company that sells to police departments and you can read about an array of security equipment that can sniff out bugs, detect phone taps, and record someone else's conversations. But you don't have to have these items to foil surveillance.

For example, if you think your phone is tapped, use common sense and avoid using it for any smuggling-related conversation. Again, even if you don't suspect surveillance, your phone shouldn't be used for anything related to smuggling except to receive a call from a pay phone telling you to go out to a pay phone and call back. If you think someone has a good reason to attempt to record a conversation with you, conduct your conversation in a sauna where no one is wearing anything but a towel. If you think your aircraft might be bugged or your aircraft transponder altered, then it gets a bit more technical and requires some expertise, but disconnecting the cable that hooks the transponder up to the outside antennae is going to prevent any "altered" transponder codes from leaving the aircraft.

Night-vision goggles and starlight scopes were talked about a lot during Operation Desert Storm, and the same ones that the military used can be purchased from private suppliers for $3,000 to $5,000. However, the use of these gadgets is very limited, and I don't think it's worth the money or the explaining you'll have to do if you are ever caught with one in your possession.

Avoiding Radar Detection

The technology exists to foil radar's effectiveness a high percentage of the time. However, this technology is not cheap, and it involves aircraft and boat design so radar beams don't bounce off directly for a good return, special paint that absorbs radar beams, and electronic countermeasures that confuse the incoming radar beams. This is all incorporated into aircraft like the F-117 or the B-2 bomber (which didn't work out to be as stealthy as the Pentagon had hoped) and is not available to the civilian population. However, there are some very simple things that can be utilized to help a boat or airplane avoid radar detection:

▶ *Paint the boat or aircraft with general house paint,* not the enamel or polychrome high-gloss paint that most repaint shops use. The F-117A stealth fighter is painted using dark, grainy, rough paint, and there is a reason for that.

▶ *Get a fuzzbuster.* It's nice to know if you are appearing on someone else's radar scopes, and the basic cop fuzzbuster will do a good job of keeping you informed. Point one forward and one aft, and if they light up two hundred miles off the North Carolina coast, I'd be thinking some AWACS plane has happened on to you.

▶ *Forget trying to jam a radar with electronic countermeasures.* They are military gadgets only and require a huge power source to operate. But don't despair—some composite-kit airplanes, such as the homebuilt Defiant, with wooden props, angled design, recessed exhaust, and fiberglass construction, are very stealthy.

Weapons

Again, *no guns.* You will win your smuggling battles by doing your homework and being prepared, not by shooting it out with law enforcement. Plus, if you are caught with a weapon in your possession while committing a felony, the sentence can be enhanced. Countries such as the Bahamas and Jamaica, which almost always have people who will accept a bribe to cancel a drug-smuggling arrest, can put you in jail just for having a handgun in your possession. Guns have no place in the smuggling business.

The essence of the drug-smuggling mission comes down to the run for the roses—getting the drug cargo into the United States. The plans and schemes to accomplish this challenge run the gamut of man's imagination. People have swallowed balloons filled with

CHAPTER 8

GETTING IN-COUNTRY

cocaine, built half-mile tunnels under the Mexican-U.S. border, and liquified cocaine to bring it in as wine. The plots, conspiracies, and schemes are endless.

That's part of the beauty of smuggling—the game constantly changes. Quick adaptation ensures continued success. That's a nice statement, but how can one know when the game is changing? The answer is to read and listen. Watch CNN, read *Time* and *Newsweek*, the *Miami Herald*, and *High Times*. Combine these with the local newspaper where you plan your area of operation, and you're going to be well informed about current happenings.

The plan used for a smuggling run should be as simple as possible and as cheap as possible. Then compare your plan to the up-to-date information available about law enforcement activities. If the plan checks out, proceed; if not, then go back to the drawing board.

For example, a friend who knows a lot of people in the Florida Marine Patrol tells me there is a big effort to intercept and search all boats coming from the Gulf Stream to the Florida inlets between Key West and Palm Beach. The effort involves coast guard patrol boats, Florida marine patrol boats, customs surveillance aircraft, and radar information. I also know from reading the *Miami Herald* that, at the time of this writing, no drug busts had been reported in the area for a few months. Putting all this information together, I can deduce that smugglers have ceded this territory to law enforcement and are attempting their smuggling runs in other areas of Florida.

There is an impressive array of money, manpower, and gadgets available to law enforcement today. But the defenses aren't insurmountable. Tactics for the early 1990s still deal with water and air. Nothing new has appeared to change the basic choice of how to get the goods in-country, and here is where I think possibilities now exist. Of course, this is not a recommendation for any specific course of action.

Remember, you and your group want to attract as little attention as possible. A smuggling group is like a stranger riding into town in the Old West—you ride in on a black horse with a silver hand-tooled saddle and everyone is going to be asking, "Who is that guy?"

Thoughts of big money and how you're going to spend it constantly float around the collective brain of a drug-smuggling group. Talking about money is a favorite activity, and the urge to "show off" by talking shit about how much money one is going to have soon has to be recognized and conquered. The collective attitude has to be "blend in; cause no one to think we're anything but hardworking, law-abiding young citizens."

This concept is not as easy as it sounds. Go out to any airport or boat marina and see how many men in their twenties or early thirties are yachting about in large boats or flying in fancy twin-engine, cabin-class airplanes. How often do three to five single guys show up in a small town in central Florida to rent an isolated house trailer? The answer is obvious. A smuggling group must understand that people are naturally curious and will ask questions, and the group should make every attempt to carry out activities in a setting and manner that will not arouse any suspicion.

There is no reason or need to travel first class or stay at expensive hotels. Take a good look at your group and try to use facilities where your appearance is in line with everyone else's.

Waterborne Smuggling

For the water smuggler in the 1990s, the trend is away from sailboats and trawlers and toward speed. This is because fewer and fewer Americans are making the long voyage down to Colombia, southern Mexico, and Belize to pick up the cargo. These trips worked great in the 1970s and early 1980s, but for an American pleasure vessel to go through the Windward Passage or Yucatan Channel now is to invite a boarding from the U.S. Coast Guard.

Mother ships still bring cargo out of the growing and refining areas, but they never go through the narrow openings on the east and west sides of Cuba. These cargo haulers head east past the Antilles and Lesser Antilles to the vast expanses of the Atlantic Ocean. Once out there they are virtually undetectable. Then they will come into the Bahamas for transshipping or continue much farther north for off-loading to American "go-fast" boats.

Unless you are well-connected in the Bahamas, it's just too risky to take a chance of getting a load there today. Besides, if you select the Bahamas as a transshipment point, you have to deal with the Straits of Florida, the ribbon of ocean between the Bahama Islands and the Florida coast that is the gem of the U.S. government's interdiction effort. This area has had special status since the mid-1980s, and there is no U.S. coast with a larger concentration of manpower and equipment to try and stop waterborne drug smuggling.

The East Coast of the United States, from Maine to the Carolinas, has overtaken Florida as the primary area of entry for drug cargos coming in by water. This area is wide open. There are no choke points, as in the Florida Straits, where traffic can be monitored, and from May through September the water off this area is a clogged freeway of boat comings and goings. If a mother ship makes a successful off-loading to a pleasure vessel in this area, it is very hard for law enforcement to sift through all the boats on any given day to figure out which one might have illegal contraband on board.

Rendezvous far out at sea, then run the stuff in. Loran and satellite navigational boxes for boats are cheap and commonplace, and for two boats to meet up at a spot in the ocean is no problem. In Newport, Rhode Island, the runner boat might be a sailboat; in Maine, a fishing boat might best do the job; for New York, a small yacht might be the best bet. A forty-foot sailboat crewed by men in their twenties and thirties is not an uncommon sight around Cape Cod. But the same boat with the same crew might cause a commotion in the Florida Panhandle Gulf Coast area.

Note: Smugglers are quick to adapt to a changing field of battle.

With the Gulf of Mexico and the coast of Florida heavily patrolled, the warriors of the 1990s who haven't switched operations to the upper eastern seaboard have moved their activities to the West Coast of the United States. This means that the use of Mexico has replaced the Bahamas as the transshipment point of choice.

A perfect business relationship between Colombians, Mexicans, and Americans is thus established. The Colombians, not wanting to send their mother ships through the Panama Canal with large drug cargos aboard, move their loading areas to the western coasts of Colombia and Ecuador. The loads are then taken by boat or airplane to Mexico and loaded onto Mexican vessels that head up the western coastline. Favorite spots for rendezvous are off Oregon and Washington, where there is a large commercial fishing fleet, plus thousands of islands and coves for unloading cargo.

Source-country smugglers are very adept at getting their cargo into position for their American counterparts to rendezvous on the open seas. *And that's the tactic that is going to be an odds-on winner for the American entrepreneurial smuggler in the early 1990s.* The fact that source-country smugglers will get the cargo in position greatly reduces the exposure that the American smuggler will have with goods on board.

For those who set up their mission so that they will be yachting to their source country to pick up the goods, the best tactic is to stay far out at sea and come in as far north as possible. Don't worry about satellite surveillance propaganda. The coast guard and navy don't have the time or money to send battleships and cutters a thousand miles to check out a boat—or even to try to find a boat—that some satellite might have taken a picture of.

Airborne Smuggling

For the airborne smuggler, the early 1990s stack up like this. Customs has its Airborne Early Warning and Control System (AWACS) planes, which, if all things are working right, can bite off two hundred miles of border per plane. Thus, if six planes are airborne at the same time, the Florida coastline could be monitored completely. The navy is deploying carrier groups in the Caribbean to try and monitor air traffic out of Colombia, and the air force uses Boeing AWACS planes to watch border areas when possible.

There is going to be a line of Aerostat balloons along the whole southern border of the United States, and over-the-horizon radar, which has been set up mainly to watch for Russian missile launches, is going to be modified to detect airplanes in the Caribbean. Even the FAA has changed its regulations so "N" numbers for aircraft have to be displayed in at least twelve-inch letters, and all aircraft flying into or out of the United States have to have a mode C transponder with altitude readout so planes can be closely monitored in the border zone.

The playing field has definitely gotten more cluttered with potential opponents. In the 1970s it didn't take a genius to come up with the tactic of flying low and keeping the transponder shut off as the way to penetrate the U.S. border. In the 1980s, law enforcement officials identified the main smuggling routes coming out of Colombia, Jamaica, and Mexico and used newly available technology (AWACS, forward-looking infrared radar, and early-alert radars) to challenge the smuggler.

My smuggling group adapted to the increased surveillance and kept the same fly-low tactic, but instead of coming up over Haiti, then the Bahamas, to enter along the east coast of Florida, we switched to flying over the Yucatan Passage then continuing north to enter the United States around Apalachicola, Florida.

The technology being deployed in the early 1990s is cause for another review of tactics by the airborne smuggler who wants to keep the odds in his favor. The main defenses are set up along the southern border and the Florida coast; that still leaves plenty of available border along the upper East and West Coasts of the United States, as well as Canada.

However, no general-aviation airplane can make the trip from the source countries (except northern Mexico) to the northern coastal borders of the United States without auxiliary fuel or a refueling stop in the Bahamas or northern Mexico. For a small entrepreneurial unit, making sure that the refueling and loading in the source country go as planned is enough of a problem. To take a chance on a second fueling stop in a foreign country is too risky a proposition, especially when that second stop will involve an aircraft that already has its drug cargo aboard. However, you can eliminate the need to deal with a second fuel stop and still avoid the well-monitored southern border areas by adding enough auxiliary fuel to your aircraft.

For the 1970s smuggling environment, the less-gas, bigger-load, short-trip tactic made sense. *For the 1990s it does not.* Before the smuggling defenses of the southeast and southwest United States were improved, it seemed foolish to head out of these areas for the landing and unloading of the airborne drug cargo. It could be effectively argued that to get to a more northern border penetration area would require an extra hundred gallons of fuel, which would equate to an extra six hundred pounds of aircraft gross weight. If you had to remove six hundred pounds of marijuana cargo (at a potential profit of $220 per pound) to compensate for the added fuel load, that loss of $132,000 just was not worth the added safety that a more northern border penetration and off-loading area provided.

However, the increased border surveillance of the 1990s has made the above argument invalid. Pick your trip profile and penetration area based on staying as far away from the bulk of the coastal defenses as possible. If your mission is busted because you challenged the strength of the antismuggling effort, whether you had 4,000 or 3,200 pounds of marijuana cargo aboard isn't going to make any difference to your well-being.

Two things available free of charge that help the airborne smuggler are clouds and thunderstorms. Clouds make it hard for a chase plane to intercept and follow; they also greatly reduce the operating area where forward-looking infrared radar and look-down radar are effective.

Thunderstorms almost guarantee that a mission will be a success. I like to see a nice, thick line of thunderstorms forecast for the smuggling route, the kind that show up on the weather channel displays as having lots of yellow and red cells present. Here's why: pilots are taught from day one to avoid thunderstorms at all costs — if you mess with the devil, bad things like wings falling off or air frames getting bent can result. Well, the bad news is that this is true; it has happened that wings have fallen off due to violent thunderstorms. The good news is that such an occurrence is very rare.

The first time you fly through an intense thunderstorm with rain pounding on your windshield like machine-gun fire and the drafts pushing you up and down like an amusement park ride will reaffirm the wisdom of your flight instructor's advise to avoid thunderstorms. He was right, of course, but then a flight instructor does not get paid multithousands of dollars a day for his efforts.

A thunderstorm offers you a sanctuary. It gives you that edge that Butch Cassidy and the Sundance Kid thought they had when they were being chased by the posse across rock-hard ground where no hoofprints could be left. Chase planes are left behind; you're hard to track.

Excellent one- to three-day weather forecasts available on cable television let you plan for mission launches at a time that will present a potential weather barrier for anyone who might be chasing you. For the 1990s flying environment, I'd rather fly through a hurricane or tropical depression than have to face a clear, cloudless route for my drug-smuggling run.

Meanwhile, an entrepreneurial aircraft designer in Mojave, California, has given the airborne smuggling community an effective new player. Dick Rutan, of Voyager nonstop, around-the-world fame, has designed a twin-engine aircraft that is available to home-builders in kit form.

The Defiant is an aircraft constructed of radar-absorbing composites that cruises in excess of 180 knots while using 18 gallons per hour. It can carry 115 gallons of fuel and has a realistic range of over 1,000 nautical miles. This is a four-seater aircraft that can carry over six hundred pounds with full fuel. If you put one two-hundred-pound pilot plus add another 50 gallons in a fuel bladder, that still leaves two hundred pounds for cargo, and that's just to bring the aircraft up to maximum take-off weight.

Composite technology means the Defiant is basically a plastic airplane that absorbs radar rather than reflecting it. The metal propeller, the single item most responsible for a radar return, is eliminated and replaced with a wooden prop. Also, the design of the aircraft is so streamlined that the exhaust ports are recessed, shielding the radar and infrared return that metal exhaust stacks provide. The Defiant is classified as a "stealth" general-aviation aircraft. Once its transponder is disconnected, it becomes the first stealth aircraft to have the availability and performance capabilities to make it a viable weapon for the airborne drug smuggler.

If the Defiant, which costs in the area of $130,000 for the kit, radios, and labor to put it together, proves popular, look for law enforcement to try to do something eventually to make the plane give a radar return.

The American military branches are now involved. That's the biggest change in the forces stacked up to stop the drug smuggler today.

CHAPTER 9

THE FORCES OF CHANGE

U.S. Army

With the army this means more military exercises along the Mexican-U.S. border. The army will also be utilized to set up mobile ground-based radars to cover suspected smuggling routes and monitor remote border locations of foreign countries. Furthermore, the army can deploy ground-sensing equipment and use all of its night-vision equipment — infrared scopes and infrared goggles.

But the army has never been known as a stealth-type organization, so if it marches into the border town of Del Rio, Texas, for a week of maneuvers looking for smugglers, the whole West Texas region will know within hours what is happening. The army can't counter that great American smuggler weapon, the telephone.

U.S. Navy

The navy has been keeping an eye out for smuggling vessels for years. It has found a loophole that allows it to stop almost any boat it wishes, and this is to carry a U.S. Coast Guard officer on board. The coast guard does have legal authority to stop and search any boat that is flying the U.S. flag or is in U.S. territorial waters within twelve miles of a U.S. coastline. This, plus the practice of stopping boats for the "hovering vessels act" (which allows any vessel in American or international waters that is suspected of off-loading illegal cargo to another boat to be detained and searched), means that you don't want to see a navy ship coming toward you.

U.S. Air Force

The air force has the greatest chance of having an impact on airborne smugglers. It has all those AWACS airplanes that are supposed to be able to put out look-down airborne radar covering three hundred miles per aircraft. The problem is that the AWACS aren't all that great at picking up small, slow, prop aircraft on their radar scopes. AWACS planes were designed as airborne radar platforms to control an air battlefield. They work pretty well in a place like Iraq, where there is little or no commercial aircraft traffic to conflict with the warplanes. However, picking out an airplane attempting to enter the United States with drugs is another matter.

In that area of operations, there are lots of commercial planes, as well as general aviation traffic. Some of these aircraft are squawking electronic codes and some aren't. Also, planes flying low and slow are often lost in ground clutter (often an aircraft flying within three hundred feet of the ground gets mixed up in the signals bouncing back off the ground and doesn't appear on the scope). Furthermore, atmospheric conditions can cause radar scopes to give erroneous readouts. In other words, AWACS airplanes can do a great job if they're stationed over the Persian Gulf, but they're another story in this part of the world.

U.S. Coast Guard

As for the coast guard, it was the first of the military branches to embrace the war against the smuggler—and the first to inform the general public about its antismuggling efforts. There was always a press release when a cutter was reassigned to the Florida area for antismuggling patrols. But in reality, aside from a few boat reassignments, the coast guard has stuck to its primary mission, and that is to help boaters in distress.

Most of the military efforts in the 1990s will just be publicized fluff. The navy will board more vessels, the coast guard will conduct more safety checks, and they all will make major claims about the impact they have on the drug smuggler. However, the military's main mission is to be ready to fight wars, and that mission will not change. The military doesn't want to be involved in a war it can't win. This happened in Vietnam, and the military leadership is not going to let the nation's defense get bogged down in a situation where it is not possible to get a clear-cut victory.

U.S. Customs

The agency a smuggler should worry about is the U.S. Customs Service. In the early 1980s, customs got an aggressive director named William Von Raab. He saw an opening to make customs the lead agency to combat drug smuggling, and he effectively pushed for equipment and manpower so he could get his agency on the point. He also used every opportunity to stress how reluctant other federal agencies were to really act. This strategy on Von Raab's part was successful, and customs grew from having two intercept aircraft in 1981 to eighty-eight intercept aircraft and helicopters in 1989. These aren't out-of-date, not-right-for-the-job machines, either; they are state-of-the-art planes and helicopters for accomplishing intercept and long-chase missions. Customs also has macho cigarette chase boats.

Customs is more flexible than the plodding military and has outfitted itself by selecting the right equipment to go after the mobile and elusive smuggler. The core of the customs antismuggling effort was spelled out in a September 9, 1985, edition of *Aviation Week and Space Technology* magazine. Look it up.

Bribery

There is one last point to mention about dealing with the vast array of local, state, and federal forces out there to stop the drug smuggler from getting goods in country—*bribery*.

Bribery is an effective tool outside the United States. However, within the United States, antidrug-smuggling personnel are generally well-paid, and the penalties for accepting a bribe are harsh. Unless you have absolute confidence in whom you are offering the money to and confidence that his information is accurate, your money will just be thrown away. Law enforcement people will be happy to listen to your offer and might even give you information to keep the conspiracy going. But the odds are that they'll report the contact to their superiors and work the case to get a bribing-a-law-enforcement-officer charge brought against you.

Obviously, successful bribes are never revealed, so there is no way to know just how much bribing of American law enforcement exists, but my guess is that it is almost nonexistent. *Don't try it.*

Off-loading Cargo

The area where I have seen the most problems with an airborne smuggling mission is the unloading of the cargo. Picking the right spot to unload, as well as working out an escape plan, means putting in the advance surveillance work so everyone on the scene knows what their jobs are and what to do if something goes wrong.

With all the remote, hardly used airports available in the United States, there shouldn't be any need to resort to a road or a field for a landing site. Two weeks of watching an airport will give you a good feel for the vehicle and air traffic that can be expected during the time you think your aircraft will be landing.

There is no such thing as being too concerned about the landing and unloading process. The unexpected will happen, and when it does it often comes down to a group member making a spur-of-the-moment judgment call to save the day.

For example, take the night Gene and I landed a DC-3 in a south Florida field. On landing rollout we hit a soft spot, and the plane came to an abrupt halt, destroying the props and damaging the fuselage. The two trucks picking up the seven-thousand-pound cargo also got stuck. That night no one had thought about the possibility of the vehicles getting stuck.

The result was that we had to leave two trucks in the field, along with the damaged DC-3, and we only got 1,500 pounds of the cargo to the safe house. If one of the twenty guys on the ground crew had understood what the job involved, he might have suggested bringing some shovels or high-axle jacks along just in case it was muddy or rainy that night. But no one sat down with the ground workers to go over the mission. The workers thought all they had to do was go unload some bales, then go home and wait for the payday.

The best you can hope for when you meet the unexpected is that all involved are trained and briefed on just what is supposed to happen and what their jobs are. If someone doesn't take the briefings and advance work seriously, then he should be replaced and not be allowed to participate.

The Chase

Another element of an airborne smuggling mission that has to be anticipated is what happens if chase helicopters and airplanes are on the smuggling plane's tail. Customs has announced that this is the way it is going to catch airborne smugglers, and there is no doubt it has the capability.

If your smuggling airplane has been intercepted, the odds are that you aren't going to know about it. Chase airplanes and helicopters do not fly up on your wing, wave at you, and point to the ground indicating you should land immediately.

A pilot might be able to figure out he is being chased by listening to the voice chatter of the center or approach-control frequency as a controller vectors traffic to move it out of the way of the smuggling and chase aircraft. A smuggling pilot can do an abrupt 360-degree clearing turn to see if anything is behind him. He can even climb up to sixteen thousand feet, which is well above the height at which the Blackhawk helicopters can operate. But none of these precautions are going to guarantee that you aren't being followed. Most likely it is going to be a ground crew member who first hears the "whop, whop, whop" of a helicopter's rotor blades, at which time he'll radio the pilot to execute the escape plan.

From the first noise of those rotor blades, the pilot has approximately three minutes to land, hook up with the ground crew, and get out of the airport, and then another five minutes to get to a public place, like a restaurant or shopping mall, where he can get lost in a crowd before a highway patrolman or local cop can intercept the getaway vehicle.

Of course, you will have to abandon the vehicle that got you to the spot where you can disappear in the crowd, and it would be helpful to have another vehicle nearby so you can continue the getaway.

Places that offer this kind of getaway potential do exist. The compromise is having to give up a rural airport for one where there is a populated public place within five or six minutes of the runway.

It used to be that the airborne smuggler hoped for a clear, star-lit night to carry out his smuggling mission. Now, clouds, thunderstorms, and bad weather are the desirable conditions. Don't forget—if smuggling were easy, everyone would be doing it; you don't get paid big money for doing something that is risk-free and requires no expertise.

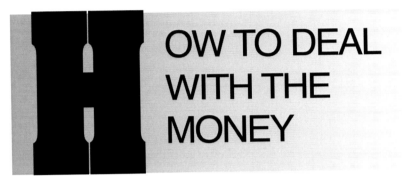

PART II

HOW TO DEAL WITH THE MONEY

If a smuggling mission has been successful and sale
gone smoothly, a person might then find himself with more
cash in his possession than he ever dreamed about. If that p
has been using the standard financial instruments of checks, credit

CHAPTER 10

REEN CASH

cards, and savings accounts, having a huge pile of cash sitting
around can be a shock.

Living a Cash Life

Salaries or profits from an illegal drug-smuggling trip don't
come with an IRS 1099 wage-earner form. This is money the government knows nothing about, and as the recipient of this
unknown money, your job is to disperse it back into the monetary
system without drawing attention to yourself.

The government doesn't have the manpower to try and figure
out which citizens are living a cash life and which aren't. The government does know that a huge underground economy exists
wherein no sales or income taxes are paid. The government also
knows that, given the opportunity, just about everyone in the
country will try to take advantage of a loophole or outright trick
the IRS out of money.

Living a cash life revolves around the concept that there be no
record of any illegally gained money you spend. That sounds like
a simple thing to do, and it is, but you may have to radically
change spending habits that have been ingrained for decades.
Think of your money as good money and bad money. Good
money comes from legal sources and is to be saved or invested in

legitimate areas. Bad money comes from illegal sources and can't be saved in the usual way of depositing it into a checking or savings account.

Bad money can be used to pay, via cash or money order, for every single aspect of your life. Bad money lets a person go about his business and takes away the one thing that law enforcement counts on the most in prosecuting drug money cases: a paper trail. If a paper trail of spending can be established, then the next step— proving that a person has no visible means of support to pay for expenditures—becomes easy. A paper trail of expenditures and purchases proves that you cannot possibly afford the life-style you lead unless you are receiving unreported money.

When most people receive a paycheck, they deposit it in the bank. From their checking account, they write checks for purchases and expenditures. If a person doesn't wish to write a check, he has the option of putting the expense on a credit card. In either case, at the end of the month a statement comes showing exactly when and on what a person has spent his money. It's all very organized.

But you aren't the only one who receives a record of your spending. The record also stays with the issuing bank or credit card company. These records are the lifeblood of law enforcement; it is easy to get a court order and subpoena financial records. Then it's even easier to ask you to explain how you spent more than $35,000 on Rolex watches at such and such a store when you haven't had a job or filed an income tax return in five years.

The object is to avoid any kind of financial investigation, and you do this by not leaving any paperwork to be investigated. First, it is important to understand that two types of investigations can result from a red flag that might have gone up regarding your financial dealings.

In the illegal drug environment of the 1990s, an investigation for alleged smuggling is going to be done with the hope of seizing assets. If the DEA or FBI develops a case, investigators will go to the U.S. attorney's office and request IRS participation in the case. By doing this at an early stage, the government is not only trying to indict an individual for criminal drug activity, it is also setting the groundwork for seizing as much of his money, assets, and property as possible. Therefore, a drug arrest or investigation can bring about close scrutiny of a person's finances.

Common red flags are U.S. Currency Transaction Form 4789 and IRS Form 8300. These forms are required by any bank or business when a cash transaction of more than $10,000 is involved. The form must be filled out within fifteen working days and is then sent directly to the IRS regional office, where you can bet that it is looked at closely. There is no quicker way to get the IRS interested in who you are than having your name on a few of these forms. For the 1990s, if the IRS had its way it would also make a currency transaction form mandatory for over-$10,000 transactions involving money orders and cashier's checks.

Every dollar you receive from a legitimate source, such as a payroll check, a birthday check from your parents, or a dividend check, should go directly into your bank account and stay there. As the money builds up, you can use it to pay for the few things you want to document.

The prime example is your house. If an investigation of your finances starts, law enforcement is quickly going to eye the possibility of seizing your house under the guise of its being a public nuisance used for illegal activity. If such a proceeding starts, it is very helpful if you can produce a canceled check that shows you made the down payment. The check itself won't convince anyone that you didn't use illegal money for the down payment, and the investigators will get a court order for your checkbook records. However, when they look at your checkbook and see legitimate deposits, it will be hard for them to make a case that the house was acquired with illegal money.

The men involved in the savings and loan scandal shed light on how millionaire bankers think when they want to protect assets from seizure—they put them in their spouses' names.

This presents some problems, and one is that you don't control those assets legally. If your house is deeded in your wife's name, then she controls it, no buts about it. Thus, it's important to take a hard look at your relationship with anyone you are thinking of using to hide your ownership of an asset.

"Good" money is special money. It is money that should never be paid out for anything other than an important purchase that can't realistically be paid for in cash. Not writing checks might be a life-style shock, but you can adjust. If using green money is difficult, as with having to pay the cable TV bill to an out-of-state company, then buy a money order to pay the bill. You can pay for almost all your month-to-month living expenses in cash and buy money orders to pay for the rest. Reconstructing a person's spending habits if they aren't detailed in a checkbook requires so much effort that law enforcement usually won't even bother to try.

When you're active in an illegal enterprise, don't surround yourself with expensive possessions. Everything you own has the chance of being taken by law enforcement. Don't buy a house or apartment; rent it.

Leasing or buying an expensive car involves more paperwork than it's worth, but buying one used is easy. A private-party seller is elated to take cash; you don't have to fill out any forms, and you can usually save yourself 20 percent over what the same used car would cost if purchased from a dealership.

When you buy anything from a store, have the salesperson put down "cash" on the receipt and not your name. Then if you need to keep the receipt for warranty purposes, put it in a place where no one can find it; otherwise, throw it away. A search that turned up a bag full of receipts could be just as damaging as one that showed the items were purchased with a personal check.

Never, ever fill out U.S. Currency Transaction Form 4789 for any reason, or provide information for IRS Form 8300. If a store says you have to fill out the form as a condition of the sale, tell them no and try another store. Always remember that any item that can be bought new at a store can also be bought used from a private party.

You only need to have one credit card, and the only reason you even need that is to rent cars and hotel rooms. If these require a credit card for deposit, make sure that the reservation people understand that you will be paying in cash and instruct them not to submit the credit card charge form.

Not only do credit card transaction records show what you used your credit card for and when, they also show where you used it.

Beware — there are other paper trails that can come back to

haunt you. Smuggler Jack bought hundreds of airline tickets all over the United States and the Caribbean and never used a credit card or check, but he greedily signed up for the mileage-plus programs offered by the various airlines. When his apartment was searched, an FBI man noticed a piece of mail from a mileage-plus program. This led to a check with five major airlines, and the FBI was able to reconstruct Jack's travel schedule for the previous four years.

Eliminate all the paper from your life. That which can't be eliminated, destroy. Hide the few receipts that you need to keep for warranty records or proof of payment. Just figure that every piece of paper you generate has the potential to be a witness against you.

Successful smuggling operations don't produce stock options or career promotions for the participants. Smuggling operations produce one thing: cash. The money appears as soon as the dealer network gets its hands on the product. Once the cash starts flow-

CHAPTER 11

WHEN THE CASH STARTS FLOWING

ing, people in the smuggling group again have to adjust to a situation and system that is under pressure to offer no services to money generated from one of the largest industries in the United States. The banks won't accept large cash deposits, they won't issue cashier's checks unless they have a background investigation of the individual, and they want paperwork for any cash transaction over $10,000. It goes on and on. But money can be dealt with, just as illegal cargos are dealt with.

Law enforcement won't tell you, but what they really love about the drug business is the cash it generates. Seizing raw drugs is of little use to the cops except for the favorable publicity it generates. It they do seize raw drugs they eventually have to burn the stuff. However, seizing money does law enforcement some real good. They still get the publicity, and they also get the chance to keep some of the cash for the individuals as well as the agencies involved. Individual cops take a little, the local agencies take a little, the government takes some, and everyone is happy.

Once the money starts to come in, the leaders of a smuggling group have to make an effort to keep the other group members up to date on who is getting paid first, how prices and sales are doing, and when that individual member can expect to get paid. There's no legal framework to fall back on to settle disputes.

You then have to think about two main areas—dispersal to the group members in the form of the salary earned and storing and moving the cash itself.

Dispersal

The thought of money, as well as the actual possession of money, causes people to do strange things. People can work hard and be total team players, and then after the goods are safely in-country, they start contemplating the money that is owed them. They begin to wonder just when they are going to see it or why another group member has already been paid and they haven't. The positive group thoughts can quickly turn to negative individual ones.

All too often, a salary deal in a smuggling group is nothing more than, "I'll pay you $25,000 for helping unload the boat and driving a car from Fort Lauderdale to Chicago." However, things go wrong, or the quality of goods isn't what it should have been, and then when it's payday, the worker who thought he was going to get $25,000 is told that the payday is going to have to be reduced to $17,000. The person who was expecting $25,000 is angry and isn't going to be quite the team player on the next deal as he was on the last one.

The smuggling business revolves around handshake deals. On my first marijuana-smuggling mission, Mick told me that my pay would be $25,000, plus a new Porsche 911, because I had been working with him directly in planning the trip and I had brought aboard a friend who was the boat expert we so desperately needed. I agreed to the salary, and we went off to successfully smuggle five thousand pounds of Colombian commercial-grade marijuana into Florida after a pickup from a mother ship in the Bahamas. Unfortunately, the 5,000 pounds we thought we had brought in turned out to weigh only 3,800 pounds. When it came payday, Mick paid me my $25,000, plus gave everyone involved in the seagoing part of the trip a $10,000 bonus. I was surprised at the bonus and thought it was a very smart move on Mick's part to share some of the $300,000 profit he had made with his loyal crew. But the goodwill that came with the bonus quickly disappeared when I brought up the subject of the Porsche. Mick said that that part of the agreement was canceled, and that I should consider the $10,000 bonus to be the car if that's what I wanted to spend it on. I was upset, and the idea that Mick wouldn't do the fair thing on future deals we might enter into began to germinate.

I would advise setting up a salary scale based on a "minimum wage" that is paid if the mission has any kind of success, along with a price-per-pound add-on. That scheme lets an employee know what his base wage will be as well as taking into account how much weight actually is distributed. I would also specify that the price-per-pound add-on only applies to goods for which the money has been received.

When the money flow starts, everyone involved in the trip begins wondering when they are going to get their share. This group includes the suppliers, the workers, and the investors. It's only fair that a person knows where he stands in the pecking order in terms of getting paid.

The people most concerned about getting their share of the money will be the source-country suppliers. Whereas workers and investors usually have a direct and often close friendship with the guy heading the smuggling group, the source-country suppliers usually know very little about the man they are fronting goods to. Often the only link they have to the head of a smuggling group is a telephone number, and they are dependent, more than anyone else, on the integrity of the smuggler they made the deal with. Since we understood their concerns about getting paid, and to establish the fact that we were impeccably honest, we would pay source-country suppliers first.

Once the source-country people are paid, the next job is to pay the workers and then pay off any investors who might have a stake. The money that comes in after this point belongs to the "owners" who put the trip together. For example, on my first boat trip with Mick we brought in 3,800 pounds of marijuana, sold at an average price per pound of $260, for a total of $988,000. From that sum, one of the first people to receive money was Mick's Colombian supplier, who had fronted the cargo to us in return for a $100-a-pound sale price if we were successful. Thus, the first $380,000 went directly to him. Then Nick paid Big Ren, Bart, and me our $25,000 salaries, as well as $60,000 to Don for being in charge of sales, plus a $100,000 salary for himself—a total salary expenditure of $235,000. The next dispersion of funds went to an investor, who was owed $30,000 for his $10,000 investment. That left the final $343,000 which belonged to Mick for his "owners" profits of the trip. From this final installment, he handed out $10,000 bonuses to the four principal employees.

A word about investors in drug smuggling trips: the initial outlay for equipment, living expenses, and the up-front cost of goods is often more than the smuggling group leader has. In the case of the above-mentioned boat trip, Mick needed $40,000 to finance the trip—$24,000 for two cigarette-type speedboats, $3,000 for a camper truck, $3,000 to rent a stash house, plus $10,000 for travel and living expenses for the group members. Mick didn't have that much money, so he had to take on an investor.

If an investor is needed, the workers on the mission team should be the first group of people who are offered an investment opportunity. If money is still needed, then you might have to offer outside investors a chance to invest in the drug-smuggling trip.

Having the workers invest in the mission is a good idea because it gives them more of a financial stake. If you have to go to outside investors, you will be opening up your operation to all kinds of threats and compromises.

Taking in such an investor should only be considered as a last resort. At least coworkers are involved in the conspiracy as deeply as you are, and they understand the risks being taken. With an outside investor, you're generally dealing with a friend or acquaintance who is either titillated by being involved in an adventurous smuggling trip or is excited about the prospect of getting a three-to-one or higher return on his money for a two-month investment period. If things work out and you can hand the guy his money, then everything is lovely. But if the mission fails and the investment is lost, get ready for the threats of being turned in to the DEA if the money isn't repaid. Most of these outside investors will rationalize that they didn't know the money was going for a drug-smuggling deal and that by threatening to turn names in to the DEA they can somehow provide enough of a scare to get their money back.

If you do have to accept outside money, the criteria should be that it is 100-percent necessary to have that money to get the mission off the ground. Then, as soon as you can finance the mission by yourself, do so.

Storage

As the illegal drugs are turned into money, the problems of where to store the cash and then how to move it arise. Just keeping hundreds of thousands of dollars in fives, tens, and twenties around creates a problem. This is money that you can't run to the police and report stolen if that should happen, and it's money that is hard to find lame excuses for if someone should stumble across it.

The solutions run the gamut from huge efforts, like floor safes installed in houses, to nothing more than hiding the money in a closet. However, what it comes down to is not keeping significant amounts of money in the most obvious place—your primary residence. This is where law enforcement will look, it's where a disgruntled worker will look, and it's where a slip-up could result in a friend or relative stumbling upon something they shouldn't know about.

I used to keep money in a typewriter case in my room at my mother's house. The typewriter was on my desk, the case had sat in the same spot for twenty years, it was easy to get to, and I thought it was a grand place to keep ready cash. Then one day a cousin wanted to borrow my typewriter, and my mother told him to go ahead and put it in the case and take it. He opened the case and found $30,000 in small bills. In situations like that it becomes a bit hard to explain why you have that kind of money lying around the house.

When it comes to storing money, there is the practical and the impractical. Impractical is burying money in the backyard and then having to dig it up every time you need to get at it. Impractical is keeping the money in a rented storage locker fifty miles from where you live.

Unless there is significant surveillance going on, a safety deposit box at the bank is as good a place as any to keep money. A safety deposit box isn't bulletproof, but when faced with the other rational options, such as keeping the money in your home or locked in the trunk of your car, it offers the most advantages.

Money stored in a safety deposit box is easy to get at and secure against everything except a court-ordered search warrant. It is rare for law enforcement to go after a safety deposit box before an arrest, but if they find evidence that one might exist after an arrest is made, then they'll get the paperwork done that is required to open it up. This will take a few days, so it is a good idea to have a cosigner on the box so he or she can remove the cash if you're behind bars.

An alternative to a bank safety deposit box is a private safety deposit box. These offer better hours for access, but you pay for this convenience with much higher rental rates.

Anyone having knowledge of where a drug smuggler keeps his money possesses information that can be turned into a "get-out-of-jail-free" card. For this reason, where you keep your money should be information that is shared with no one. If you feel that someone has to be able to retrieve your cash if you're in jail, then limit the "need-to-know" to your wife or a trusted immediate family member. Never give your money storage information to anyone even remotely involved in any illegal activities.

The handling of large sums of cash money provides some of the truly dumb anecdotes about the smuggling business.

After Mick's and my first success in the go-fast boats, I left our Fort Lauderdale base of operations for a week to begin preparations for another mission. When I got back, Mick calmly showed me a suitcase in his hotel room that contained $560,000 collected from the sale of our marijuana. He had a gun in the suitcase, and he left me with the cash and the gun while he went to buy pizza and beer for dinner.

I sat in that hotel room and just stared at the money. Having that much money in my immediate grasp was like being told I was leaving for a trip to Mars in twenty minutes; I wasn't ready for it.

For two days I watched Mick bring the suitcase with us as we drove about Fort Lauderdale doing business. He had no worries about dragging around that huge sum of cash. I, on the other hand, couldn't get my mind off it. How Mick could be so lackadaisical about this small fortune amazed me.

Carelessness with money was typical of Mick. He once left a briefcase with $80,000 stored in the overhead storage bin of a commercial airliner. He realized he had forgotten the briefcase just after he had claimed his luggage; he got back to the gate just before the airliner was pulling out.

Another time we had to deliver a $280,000 backside payment to the Colombians in Nassau, Bahamas. Mick put the two packages containing this money on the back of a motor scooter he had rented. He was driving the scooter flat out, as usual, and when he flew over a speed bump the packages jarred loose and fell off.

We got to the hotel and had no packages. We retraced our route, and there, neatly stacked on the side of the road, were two packages. A local Bahamian gardening nearby saw Mick picking up the packages and told him that he had seen them fly off and stacked them up nicely for his return. Mick tipped the man $100 and we sped off. After these incidents, Mick let me be in charge of the money whenever we were together.

Once the cargo has been off-loaded successfully in-country and dispersed to the sales organizations, a smuggling group goes into a week or two of limbo while it waits for the money to start rolling in. During this period it's hard to get group members to relax because of the anticipation of the upcoming payday.

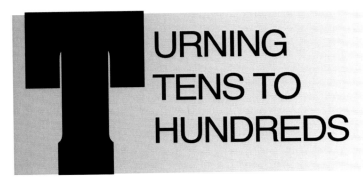

CHAPTER 12

TURNING TENS TO HUNDREDS

By the time the money did start to appear, my smuggling group leader, Mick, would then insist that we get out of the motel rooms and the boredom of sitting around watching TV, to go out and change all the money into fifties and hundreds. Not only did this relieve the boredom and demonstrate trust in the workers by giving them a lot of money to be responsible for, it also made the cash much easier to transport and store.

Mick would parcel out the small bills, and off we would go to the banks to convert the small bills into large ones. It also gave us a weird psychological boost to have all those $5,000 stacks of $100 bills in our possession. Mick and I both were hooked on the premise that smugglers should only deal in hundreds.

There was no part of the smuggling business I disliked more than going into a bank and asking the cashier to please change $9,000 in tens and twenties into hundred-dollar bills. We never went in with more than $9,000 on our person because we didn't want to have to deal with the $10,000 IRS reporting form mentioned earlier. However, even though I was breaking no law, I always felt that I was walking in with a red flag in my hand that said "smuggler."

Even though most bank cashiers are innocent young ladies under thirty, awareness of hundred-dollar bills is so great there was no excuse I could give that made any sense as to why I was asking for this exchange. "I own a Christmas tree lot and need to be able to keep the money in my pocket" didn't have any conviction in it.

My hatred of money changing was proven to be justified by a disastrous episode that happened to Mick after we had successfully brought in 4,500 pounds of commercial Colombian marijuana in a DC-3 aircraft.

One of the main buyers of the load was in Boston, and Mick and his brother, Big Ren, had gone there to pick up money. They had collected $360,000, and the buyer told them that if they waited around for three more days he would have another $200,000 for them. Mick decided to wait, and to kill time for the extra days, he and Big Ren would make the rounds of the downtown banks.

They changed money at several banks and went back the next day for another round of changing. At one bank a teller recognized Big Ren. Ren is six feet four inches tall and weighs more than 350 pounds, so he presents an image that one isn't likely to forget. The teller alerted the head cashier, who quickly made a call to the Boston police. After the change was complete, Mick and Big Ren got back into their rented car. They had driven two blocks when they were pulled over by a Boston detective. He made Mick open up the trunk, where he found all the money that Mick had collected—more than $360,000—in a piece of luggage.

The detective took $20,000 for himself and let Mick keep $10,000, but the bulk of the money, upwards of $330,000, was confiscated by the Boston police. The search was illegal; no charges were filed, and eventually Mick won a court case that got him back $100,000, which was all that was left once taxes and attorney fees were deducted. But this affair was a disaster. All that money was lost just to convert good money into bigger bills for storage, transport, and ego.

Today, banks have made it much more difficult to walk in off the street and change small bills into large ones. In the 1990s, banks require you to have an account with them, show ID, sign a ledger, and take an oath that the money is not drug-related; they even want to chemically test the money for traces of cocaine.

Fives and tens, when added up to total $100, work just as well as a hundred-dollar bill. It might take longer to count, take more room to store, and be bulkier to transport, but going to all the effort to add another layer of risk by changing the money from small bills to large ones is sheer foolishness.

Whether it's picking up cash from a person who has sold goods, paying off source-country people, or getting money to workers and investors, the handling of money is a hot potato.

CHAPTER 13

MOVING MONEY

Moving Money within the United States

The easiest and cheapest way to move money around in the United States is simply to mail it, either using the postal service or one of the overnight delivery services. The postal service is considered so reliable for delivering packages that most whole-sale diamond traders ship their goods uninsured. However, cash is a bit different.

Postal employees are very adept at spotting a letter or package that might contain cash. The shape of the envelope, the feel of what is inside, the weight of the package — all this and more comes into play if the experienced postal employee is of the mind to try and enrich himself by tampering with the U.S. mail. You don't hear about this kind of tampering very often, but it is a problem with the postal service, and it's something a person who plans to send cash through the mail should be aware of.

If you want to send money through the mail, the key is pack-aging and labels. Start off by selecting an object of some size that you can buy cheap at a second-hand store. I'd always use either a pair of shoes or a small appliance. Then package the object, along with the money you want to send, in a high-quality box, sealing it with fiber tape, and package that box in another strong cardboard outer box using a paper or popcorn filler. Seal the outer box with brown wrapping tape, and then you have a strong container that is going to take some effort to break into.

A nice touch that's worth the effort is to have professional-looking mailing labels printed. Using a shipping label that says something like "Sunshine Hair Care Products" or "High-Country Catalog Wholesalers" also gives a package a nice profile and makes it feasible for you to insure it for $100, saying it contains shampoo or body lotion. You don't want to insure the package for $50,000 or send it registered mail, since that just attracts undue attention. If you do decide to insure the package, realize that a person at the other end is then required to sign for the receipt, and that would leave a paper trail.

An alternative is to take your package to a mail-drop service or professional packager and have them do the double boxing while you watch and then use their shipping label.

Even though using the mail to move money around sounds very simple and safe, there still is something about having a large sum of money out of your direct control that makes mailing unacceptable. Also, one of the best parts of the smuggling business is paying out or accepting money after a successful trip. Face-to-face get-togethers involving money are usually happy times and perfect opportunities to talk over new adventures. When you're picking up $100,000 from someone or handing over $75,000 to the pilot who flew a successful mission for you, everyone involved is going to be in a good mood. This sets up a good atmosphere to bring up any problems that might exist or to go over how the last operation was carried out.

Trains and buses are safer than cars for moving money. You don't have to worry about fluke traffic stops or car breakdowns, you don't have to deal with security checkpoints as at an airport, and you can easily dress to fit right in with the bus- or train-going public. However, most people will feel that a bus or train trip of longer than four or five hours is too slow a means of transportation. That will leave what is the most popular means of getting money moved about the country: airplanes.

There is no safer way to move money or, for that matter, illegal drugs, around the United States than in a private airplane that is owned and flown by a member of the group. But this is a luxury few smuggling groups can afford. If the group uses an aircraft for the mission, that plane should be thought of as the most sacred of possessions and should not be flown about the country to pick up and drop off money. If the group can afford to own an airplane to be used for chores other than smuggling runs, that is about as bulletproof as money transfers can get. It is extremely rare for a private pilot flying his own airplane to ever be bothered by law enforcement at an airport.

However, when all factors are considered, the best way by far to move money around is via commercial airlines. The money stays in your possession, the cost of an airline ticket is reasonable, travel is fast, and weather or mechanical delays rarely happen. But using airlines to move money still presents some hurdles one needs to be aware of.

Profile

The first place the term "profile" was used in relation to drugs was at the nation's airports. The "drug courier profile" came out of the Miami DEA's office. The traits they were watching for were the usual: young, sporting a moustache and long hair, buying a one-way ticket or a round-trip ticket with travel on the same day, wearing gold chains or bracelets, having little or no luggage, paying cash for a ticket, and traveling alone.

The drug-courier profile was challenged in court on the premise that it was in violation of the U.S. Constitution for law enforcement to stop people just because of their appearance. But amazingly, the Supreme Court of the United States of America upheld the legal use of a drug courier profile by law enforcement.

Countering the use of the drug courier profile should be a concern of people moving money or illegal drugs on commercial airliners. First off, never buy your airline ticket at the airport, and don't check any bags. It's at the ticket counter that a ticket agent might suspect something and call law enforcement. If you buy your ticket at a travel agency and do not check any bags, you can avoid the ticket counter completely. Also, buying your ticket through a travel agent makes it easy to pay cash and even use a fake name for ticketing. When paying cash for a ticket at an airline ticket counter, I've been asked to show an ID (I told them I didn't have one on me), but that has never happened in my fifteen years of dealing with travel agents.

Once you have your ticket, the goal is to dress to fit in with the traveling public. Look at people in airports—you don't see too many tanned men with long hair and moustaches who are wearing three-piece suits and carrying briefcases. If you want to look like a tourist, then bring a tennis racket along or a snorkel and fins. Your endeavor is not to fit a courier profile and to look like an average member of the traveling public instead.

Where to Stash the Cash

Where to carry the money itself is the biggest problem of traveling on the airlines. Every airport with scheduled airline flights has a security or metal-detector checkpoint. It's always an anxious time, walking through that metal detector, and you certainly don't want to have some dumb oversight on your part cause a security employee to request that you open your bags or submit to a pat-down search.

Security X-ray machines are low dosage and show how dense objects in a suitcase or purse are. Metal objects are the most dense and stand out clearly on the screen, but other objects with high density also give an X-ray image that the reader can identify. Cords from appliances, soles of shoes, and books are just as identifiable.

Unfortunately, a stack of money will also show up on the X-ray screen. A $5,000 stack of twenties shows up as a mass. Since it doesn't appear as metal on the screen, and since it has a very innocent shape, few security personnel will question what it is. However, even the remote chance that a security machine operator would request that the suitcase be opened was enough to make me want to avoid having money in my carry-on luggage.

The alternative is having money on your person. The metal-detector arch is a magnetic field with an alarm. But money has nothing metallic in it, and you can walk through with thirty pounds of currency stuck in your pockets and no alarm goes off. You can tape money to your body or stuff it inside your cowboy boots, and as long as you don't look like you have strange bulges you won't be stopped.

While concealing square-shaped packets of money isn't exactly a high-tech science, it is something that must be given some thought.

If the weather is moderately cold, always wear an overcoat, ski jacket, or raincoat over your other clothes. These will muffle the outline of your inner clothes. The outfit that always worked for me was a lightweight nylon ski coat with a hood that had a built-in zipper compartment in the back. I would put on the coat and could pack in $100,000 worth of twenties. The $5,000 packages of twenties would add a padded look to my back, but to offset that I wore a dark, lightweight raincoat over the nylon ski jacket. This ensemble was comfortable since the weight of the money was distributed across my back.

If you like to be attired more stylishly as you move money about the United States, it is not hard to have a money vest made. A money vest is nothing trickier than a strong undergarment with compartments where you can stick packets of cash. Over the vest you can wear a dark, oversized shirt, and over that a jacket, and away you go.

Another option is to have a custom-made overcoat with a lining constructed so that packets of cash fit into compartments. Any tailor should be able to make one so that an observer would have no idea that the lining of the overcoat is carrying fifty to eighty pounds of cash.

There are times when there is more cash than can fit on your person, and then you'll have to put the extra in your carry-on luggage. This luggage will go through the X-ray scanner, and the outline will show up as a dense, rectangular, nonmetal object. If you have too many bills tightly packaged together, a finely tuned X-ray scanner will show a picture of the face of the bills, so don't make your packages too large.

The security people who operate X-ray scanners aren't really looking for packages of money, and you can improve your chances of not being asked to open a suitcase by keeping the packets of money less than three inches thick and using paper wrappers instead of thick rubber bands. Also, have the packets scattered about in your luggage. For example, put separate money packets inside your tennis shoes, then stuff in a sock to conceal the money from view. Wrap a shirt around a stack or stuff a bundle down the leg of a folded pair of jeans. This little bit of effort will help to divert attention from rectangular bundles in your luggage.

It goes without saying that you don't want to have anything in your carry-on bag that is made of metal. The same goes for wearing big silver buckles or carrying a knife that doubles as a key chain. You want to walk through the metal detector without setting off any alarms.

Inevitably, the time will come when a security person wants to see inside your luggage or give you a going-over with the hand-held metal detector. It happened to me twice—once when I had $50,000 in a canvas seabag between two folded Navajo rugs and once when my pockets bulged a bit too noticeably.

You do not have to consent to a pat-down search. If the security person starts to pat you down without asking your consent, step back and immediately inform him or her that you're outraged and to get his or her hands off you immediately. The security person will not allow you to proceed down the concourse, and you'll have to take your carry-on luggage and retreat, but you will have protected the money you're carrying.

Airport security personnel are not law enforcement officers; however, even law enforcement must ask your permission before patting you down for metal objects. Whether it's a policeman, DEA, or airport security, the answer is the same—do not ever consent to a search of your person, car, luggage, or house anywhere, at any time.

If a security person asks you to open your luggage for a further check, again, you do not have to comply. You can say no. If you do say okay and open your bag, then anything security wants to look at is fair game. It might be embarrassing to have a public confrontation, but once again, the higher priority is protecting the money you are carrying. It is far better to take your luggage and leave the airport than to subject your money to what can happen if someone wants to know what you're doing with $50,000 in fives and tens in your luggage. No matter what you answer, security will call the airport police detachment, and you are then well on your way to having your money confiscated.

Moving Money Out of the United States

When it comes to moving money out of the United States to your source-country supplier, it should be crystal clear to all concerned that if anything happens it is the supplier's money that is gone, not the smuggling group's.

The best way to get money to source-country people is to have them pick it up in the United States. Then they can get it transferred to wherever they want. Once that is established, then you can offer favors if you happen to be in the mood for a vacation to their tropical paradise.

If you must take money out of the United States to a source country or a Caribbean money-laundering center, follow these guidelines:

▶ *Don't take more than $100,000 at a time*, and try to conceal as much as possible on your person.

▶ *Travel with the outward appearance of a tourist and not a businessman.* If you're under thirty, take your wife or girlfriend. If you take your children, that really adds a nice touch.

▶ *Do not use your passport to establish U.S. citizenship unless a passport is required by the country you are visiting.* You can enter Mexico and all the Caribbean countries by showing your birth certificate and a picture ID, but Colombia and the other South American countries require a passport for entry. This isn't that big a deal unless one day you are detained and your passport is perused. If customs or the DEA sees a lot of trips into countries like Mexico, Jamaica, or the Bahamas, that will definitely increase their curiosity.

▶ *Avoid flying out of Miami.* Miami International is an airport where every airline employee as well as every law enforcement officer is thinking about and looking for drugs and drug money. If you're going to the Bahamas, depart through Orlando or Atlanta.

For Jamaican travel, leave through New Orleans, and for Mexico, Houston or Los Angeles will work.

In the 1990s, the trend will be to deliver payoff money to Europe. This will be helpful for both parties. European banking offers more secrecy and laundering possibilities than Nassau, the Cayman Islands, or Panama, and this safety of funds is just as important to a source-country supplier as it is to a smuggler in the United States.

In addition, the risk of detection will be less. Flights to Europe tend to leave from large northern cities, and law enforcement officials at these departure points aren't as in tune to dealing with "profiles" as they are in Miami. European customs are set up with "declare" and "nothing-to-declare" entry procedures. If you have nothing to declare, the odds of having your luggage searched are about one in thirty. Even if you do, European customs officials aren't looking for money so they can shake you down for some of it. It is not illegal to bring U.S. money into Europe, nor is it illegal to have large sums in your possession.

One thing to avoid when taking money into Europe is flying directly into the banking-center airports of Geneva and Zurich, Switzerland, as well as to Liechtenstein. Another European banking center is Luxembourg, but this small country has an airline that offers budget fares nonstop from many northern cities in the United States. So many travel agents and tour operators use Icelandic Air that a ticket-counter operator in the States would not think there was anything unusual about a Luxembourg destination.

It is far better to enter Europe where most of the tourists do, and that is via London or Paris. From these two cities it's easy to catch a train to your destination. Once you're on a train or bus it is common to have your passport checked as you enter another country, but it is very rare to have your luggage looked at. As of 1992, when the European Economic Community rules went into effect, these border checks disappeared altogether.

Another good reason to enter Europe through London or Paris is that your passport is only stamped at the point of entry into Europe. Thus, if your airline ticket to and from Europe and your passport stamp don't show a visit to the main banking countries of Switzerland, Luxembourg, or Liechtenstein, the U.S. authorities will have no inkling that you've been there unless you tell them.

A dangerous thought develops when you've made a lot of money in the drug business: you've got all this money lying around in cash, and it's not earning any interest; you should invest it. Thinking that illegal money is easy to invest leads to trouble.

CHAPTER 14

SOCK IT SOMEWHERE

Getting money earned illegally into the legal money system takes careful planning and time. It's a problem most people would love to have, and as with most problems, there are answers.

It is imperative to remember that illegal money comes into your possession tax-free. The federal government gets no share of it; nor does the state government. Together, these two taxing agencies would take in the area of 40 percent of your drug dollars if they were legal taxable income. This doesn't mean that you can't report the money on your income tax—you can. You can list your profession as drug smuggler and say you made $100,000, and then pay tax on that amount. Your IRS returns are supposed to be totally confidential. Don't count on it.

Figuring the inflation rate at 6 percent, it would take approximately five years for your tax-free money to shrink to where it would be if you had paid federal and state taxes on it. Keep this initial tax edge in mind to put into perspective how much more valuable this money is than taxed money in the first place.

With a banking system that doesn't want to handle illegal cash and a law enforcement system that is dedicated to seizing money and assets first and asking questions later, drug money has to be invested with prudence, otherwise it is far better just to let it sit— and shrink in value according to yearly inflation figures.

Nevertheless, there are thousands of plans that can be used to turn stagnant green money into productive money. The most conservative of these plans involves dealing with a reputable foreign bank. Just because U.S. banks won't handle "bad" money doesn't mean that there aren't other banks in the world that would be more than happy to do so.

Some countries have developed a national banking charter that specifically indicates that their intent is to provide a place where questionable monies can enter the world banking system.

There are a variety of reasons for discreet banking opportunities to exist. People are trying to avoid taxes, hide assets from spouses, and shield funds from lawsuits or bankruptcies. The world banking system needs outlets where questionable currency can be invested. This system is based on the belief that it's a far better evil to have the $5 billion stolen from the Philippines by Imelda and Ferdinand Marcos in the pipeline as capital for new ventures and jobs than have it sitting under a mattress somewhere generating nothing.

Banks in foreign countries operate under the banking laws set up by the individual country. The Chase Manhattan Bank in Nassau, Bahamas, operates under the banking secrecy laws of the Bahamas. Switzerland, Luxembourg, Liechtenstein, the Cayman Islands, and the Bahamas are best known for having banking systems with strict secrecy laws. The secrecy laws of these countries don't mean that your funds are 100-percent safe from disclosure, but they do make it very hard for an investigating agency to find information unless they have iron-clad proof that such-and-such funds from such-and-such account were gained illegally.

The last thing a country that bills itself as a safe, secret haven for funds wants is for its secrecy laws to be penetrated by an arm of some law enforcement agency. If that happened, people would quickly lose confidence and take their money to another country. There has been recent publicity about how countries that offer secret banking opportunities have capitulated to the strong arm of U.S. investigations. There is some truth to this.

If a law enforcement agency can offer precise evidence about illegally gained funds deposited to a secret account, then it is possible for the country involved to cooperate in an investigation and possible seizure. However, this is very rare and usually occurs in the few cases that offer a high degree of publicity or are politically motivated.

Money entering the legal banking system of a country with banking secrecy laws must be delivered in cash. Cashier's checks, money orders, and wire-transferred funds leave a paper trail. If the money enters a bank in Switzerland as green cash, then all that exists is a deposit slip that you immediately throw away. There is no other way to assure a safe start for your illegal money in the legal banking system.

In a good-natured conversation with a friend who happens to be a U.S. attorney assigned to the drug task force as a money-laundering expert, I was told about all the high-tech, sophisticated ways that have been developed for tracking and seizing suspected drug money. I had one question: "What can you do if cash currency leaves the United States and then is deposited in a country that has banking secrecy laws?" The answer from the money laundering expert was, "That's a problem."

It is impossible to do much about people taking cash out of the country. Customs has the right to question and search people leaving the United States to determine whether they are departing with more than $10,000, and you are supposed to fill out a currency and monetary instrument report, just as you would when bringing more than $10,000 in. However, these defenses do little good. Instead, efforts have focused on applying pressure to the countries with banking secrecy laws not to accept cash deposits of American currency.

Pressure, when applied by the world's biggest economy and strongest military power, is not a joke. In the 1970s and 1980s there was no easier place to do confidential banking business than the Bahamas. The banks there would accept any cash deposit for a modest 1 percent of the transaction fee, and the country hadn't been as prosperous since prohibition days—the prime minister was able to build and live in a $3 million mansion on his $40,000-a-year salary.

The change came in the late 1980s. In exchange for lighter sentences, a lot of people began offering up testimony that the prime minister of the Bahamas was a big player in the drug-smuggling action. The resulting investigations and publicity caused the elephant (the United States) to tell the mouse (the Bahamas) that his antics were tiresome and that if he wanted to survive, change must come. The prime minister got in a final shot when the population reelected him in spite of all the allegations of bribery and smuggling involvement, but he knew that the freewheeling days were over. He saw the light and accepted increased DEA aid in the form of advisers and equipment. He also maneuvered the banking charter to make it much easier for U.S.-initiated drug investigations to gain access to Bahamian records. Furthermore, Nassau banks began to refuse to accept deposits of U.S. cash.

The best answer to getting money into a productive mode involves the area of the world where the concept of secret banking was invented, one that has almost a sixty-year history of confidentiality. That area is Europe, more specifically, the countries of Switzerland, Luxembourg, and Liechtenstein.

Banking secrecy developed in the 1930s in Europe because the people didn't have faith in their countries' tax policies or currency. They would be paid for goods and services, and rather than putting the money into the local banking system to keep it circulating, they would hide it to avoid taxes and bank failures. What developed was a situation where too high a percentage of the European currencies simply disappeared from circulation. The result of this disappearance of capital, plus the political instability caused by the rise of Nazi Germany, crippled the economy of the whole region. From this mess arose Switzerland's banking secrecy laws.

Switzerland had been a totally neutral country, a nonparticipant in wars or alliances, and it offered a banking system wherein transactions could be conducted in complete secrecy. Thus evolved the famous Swiss secret-numbered account. Europe accepted Switzerland's banking system because even though it was obviously a haven for people trying to avoid taxes or hide assets, the alternative—the loss of the money from the system—was worse.

Switzerland's banking system is the backbone of its prosperity, a prosperity that has given it the highest standard of living of any country in the world. Word has it that even the start-up in 1992 of the European Economic Community is not going to change drastically the way the Swiss handle bank accounts.

Switzerland has felt the most pressure surrounding drug-money investigations because it is by far the world's biggest secret banking center. There are now provisions in the banking charter of Switzerland that allow the United States, if it wants records, to present its case to the Swiss government. A bank might then be allowed to release the specific records requested. However, this is complicated and time-consuming, involving multiple layers of bureaucracy. The Swiss only go along with U.S. requests a few times a year, and, as mentioned previously, these cases are always big media events that receive lots of publicity.

Of more concern is the May 1991 announcement that Switzerland would abolish its Form B accounts, which allowed transactions to be conducted through a lawyer, notary, or trust administrator so clients never had to reveal their identities—just another example of U.S. pressure being exerted. However, this is a very small loss when taken in the context of all the possibilities that European banking secrecy offers, and the 1990s won't bring anything other than lip service in regard to U.S. efforts to break down the confidential guarantees of the banking systems of Switzerland, Luxembourg, and Liechtenstein.

European banks and investment houses are in business to make money, just as those in the United States. However, there are some distinct differences to be aware of. In all my trips into banks there, I never saw anyone dressed more casually than a suit and tie. The first time I entered a bank in Switzerland, I was wearing shorts, a polo shirt, and a raincoat. I was scrutinized like I was a clown from the circus. Save yourself an anxiety attack and wear a dark suit and a tie to do your European banking.

Another difference between European and American banks is that absolutely nothing fazes the discreet European banker. Walk into an American bank to deposit $200,000 in twenties, and 99 percent of the tellers will gasp and run for a supervisor, who will, in turn, gasp and run for the FBI. In Europe, your money is accepted, counted, and deposited right there. It's just another ordinary transaction to the tellertrons at a Eurobank.

Your choice of a foreign bank depends on what kind of service you want. The options range from full-scale banks doing business in many countries, like Credit Suisse or Citibank, to one-room private-investment banks. If your desire is to merely deposit money

CHAPTER 15

YOU DON'T NEED THE BCCI

and let it earn interest, the best place is one of the bigger banks. If you're looking to play games and move the money around a bit to reintroduce it into the United States, you are probably better off with a small investment bank where you can establish a close working relationship with an individual. Either way, there are really only three questions you need to ask:

▶ "Can I set up a confidential, numbered account?"

▶ "Will you accept U.S. dollars in unlimited cash quantities?"

▶ "What is your deposit fee?"

If the first two questions are answered to your satisfaction, the only thing left is the deposit transaction fee. A fee in the area of 1 percent is to be expected at European banks. However, a deposit fee of 3 percent and up is the first indication that a bank is nervous about cash deposits.

When you first walk into a European bank and ask about a "numbered" secret account, there may be some confusion as to what you want. This is because there is no such thing as a numbered account that doesn't have a name attached to it in some way.

What makes these accounts seem secret to Americans is that there is no paper trail and, therefore, no information (e.g., a Social Security number matched to an account number) can be given to any government agency, such as the IRS.

When you open a European account, you have to fill out a name and address form, and the bank will probably make a photocopy of your passport. Then you are issued an account number, which can be considered your secret banking code. From then on the bank only does business with you by account number. You don't need to put your name on deposit or withdrawal forms.

It's an unnatural experience to leave a chunk of your money in a foreign bank and then destroy all the paper links you have to that money. However, this is what you have to do. Your account number must be committed to memory. As a backup, you might have the account number engraved on the back of a watch or a piece of jewelry, or stamped to look like a serial number on an appliance you travel with.

The three big "don'ts" associated with foreign accounts are: don't call the bank from your home phone, don't bring bank deposit slips or correspondence through U.S. Customs, and don't make deposits or withdrawals from your "secret" account at any bank branch other than the one where it's set up. It goes without saying that if you tell more than one trusted relative who is not in the drug business about your account, its "secret" status is greatly diminished.

If you must call your European bank from the United States, you'll have to go to a pay phone with rolls of quarters. If your phone records are ever subpoenaed and law enforcement finds a call to Switzerland, Luxembourg, Liechtenstein, the Cayman Islands, or the Bahamas, you can bet that they will follow up to see if that phone number is associated with a bank. It is far better to show up at your bank in person, tell them you want to make a withdrawal, and then come back when they have the cash to give you, than to make a phone call from the States to Europe to tell the bank to get the cash ready for your arrival. Also, phone numbers in an address book or on a Rolodex file give away secrets just as quickly as if they're printed out on your telephone bill.

Don't-carry-it paperwork includes a business card from your European banker, a deposit slip, a readout of your current balance, and a readout of how your funds are invested. Customs, if they get interested in you, know all the places where a piece of paper can be hidden, and that includes your pooper chute. Plus, if you think customs will just ask a few questions when they find a business card for a European bank rolled up into the sleeve of a dirty shirt, you're wrong. It will be the start of a very unpleasant experience that is guaranteed to give you a place of honor in their master computer for the rest of your life.

Regarding the third big "don't," Bank of America has a very nice facility in Nassau, where you can set up a "secret" account, and if you go to the Bank of America in San Francisco, you can have your account records accessed and make a deposit or withdrawal. However, since the United States doesn't have bank secrecy laws, the San Francisco branch will ask you for your Social Security number, since it operates under U.S. banking rules, and not those of the Bahamas. Banking only where your "secret" account is set up ensures that private information doesn't find itself in some computer that can be accessed by an unfriendly government agency.

Getting Your Money Out

Half the challenge is getting your money happily tucked away in a foreign bank account; the other half is getting that money out. The obvious answer is to withdraw it and bring it back in cash. However, to reenter the United States you have to go through U.S. Customs. The reentry customs declaration asks whether you have more than $10,000 in cash or financial instruments (i.e., cashier's checks, traveler's checks, money orders, etc.) in your possession. If you answer yes, then the customs officer will want to know how much, whether you took that much out of the country with you (which is illegal unless you filled out a declaration), and, if you didn't take that much out, where you got it. Plus, answering yes on the form will mean a computer check of your name as well as a search of your luggage and person.

If you don't answer yes and the customs people find more than $10,000 on you, the burden of proving it's legitimate income is going to be heavy. Saying that you won the money in Monte Carlo or found a gold Rolex on the beach and sold it isn't going to work. If you're caught with the money and you haven't declared it, the only question is going to be whether customs seizes the whole amount or requires you to pay a hefty fine.

Yes, you can take your five best friends on a trip to Europe and give them each $9,999 to bring back through customs, but, if you're discovered, customs isn't going to be impressed with your knowledge of the monetary entry laws. Chances are that the person who is stopped will give up the whole ship and tell customs exactly what it wants to know. If that includes which bank the money came from, then your whole motherlode is at risk.

People are often advised that if they are wearing an expensive watch or taking an expensive camera or video recorder with them on an out-of-country vacation, they should register the item with U.S. Customs before departure from the United States. Then, when they come back through customs they can show the paperwork. A creative thinker might get the idea that he can buy ten counterfeit Phillipe Patek gold watches and register them with customs on his outgoing flight. Then he can throw the watches away in Europe and take $30,000 of his "secret" money to another European bank and have a cashier's check issued with the remitter being "Paris Antique Watches." When coming back through U.S. Customs he can declare the $30,000 cashier's check as payment for the ten "antique gold watches."

The above method could be tried with any kind of jewelry, furs, art, or personal items appraised at over $10,000. However, customs employees aren't fools, and it is very rare that someone will go waltzing out of the country, register a selection of watches or diamonds, and then come back through customs declaring a large cashier's check. If you're fifty-five years old with wealthy parents who recently died, this move might be plausible. However, if you're young and your name is already in the computer for suspected smuggling activity, you haven't a snowball's chance of getting that declared cashier's check into the United States without producing receipts and depositions from whomever you sold the merchandise to.

So how, then? The best way is to avoid the old-hand customs officers, and that means avoiding airport customs. That leaves boats, trains, and motor vehicles as common modes of reentry.

Taking a boat back from Europe is an expensive, time-consuming, and sophisticated way to travel. Customs knows that the more rich people present, the higher the chance that tricks are being played, thus the closer the scrutiny. Therefore, don't consider the *QE2* as a vehicle to bring your bundle of cash back to the U.S. If you want a boat ride back, book passage on a beat-up, cheap-ticket freighter.

It is not unusual for Americans to book round-trip European airline flights from the departure points of Toronto and Montreal; often the fares are a few bucks cheaper. You can enter Canada with just a proof-of-citizenship ID and reenter the United States from there with the same. To take a bus, train, or automobile back from Canada to the United States decreases the odds of U.S. Customs finding your excess cash. Another way is to land in Toronto from Europe and then have someone pick you up in a car with U.S. plates and drive the six hours to Windsor, Canada, to enter the United States at Detroit. More than likely, customs will do nothing but look in the car and wave you through without even asking you to fill out an entry form.

Much of what customs is looking for involves profiles and deviation from common sense. If you come through a northern customs stop at a peak period and you're driving a car with U.S. plates, have very little luggage in the trunk, and don't look like a revolutionary, you're probably going to get waved through. If you don't, you're probably still okay because the last thing customs will be looking for is money.

Far safer—and much more economical—than bringing your "secret" money back into the United States $9,999 at a time, is to bring it back within the framework of the laws that exist. Money laundering is a worldly profession, and the schemes involved are as varied and clever as those of smuggling itself.

For example, the "Dutch Sandwich," with its hundreds of variations, is a virtually bulletproof way to bring "bad money" back to the United States. The whole plan starts with cash deposits into an account in a country with banking secrecy laws. From there, a corporation is set up in Holland, and a trust company is set up on the island of Curacao, which is part of the Netherlands Antilles, which also has banking secrecy laws. The person who controls the "secret" account also controls the trust company in the Antilles and the corporation in Holland. The Antilles has corporate secrecy laws as well as banking secrecy laws that prevent the owner of the holding company from being revealed.

The term "sandwich" comes from the fact that the Antilles, with their corporate secrecy laws, is the conduit used to funnel the money back into the United States. This happens when the cash from the "secret" European account is transferred to the corporate account in Holland. Then it is moved to the trust company in the Netherland Antilles, where it is then loaned to the individual who brought the "bad money" over to nest in a European "secret" account in the first place. If this person has any trouble with the IRS about where all this money is coming from, the safety net is that he can point to the legitimate loan from a European corporation doing business at a major European bank. But money-laundering schemes involve hiring bankers and lawyers to set things up, so you need to be working with sums well into six figures to make it cost-effective.

There are simpler ways to move sums over $10,000 and under $200,000 back into the United States from a European "secret" account with relative safety. Most anything that can be bought in the United States can also be bought in Europe. For example, if you're planning to buy a new car, buy the car in Europe and pay for it with money from your "secret" account. Then make a vacation out of driving the car about Europe so that you can bring it back into the United States as a used car. Once the vehicle is licensed and titled, you can sell it, often making a few bucks more than you paid for the car for your importing efforts.

This plan of using your European "secret" account funds to pay for costly items you might want and then bringing the goods back to the United States can work for anything from furniture to clothing to jewelry and even art. Any piece of art or furniture that is over one hundred years old is considered an antique and therefore isn't subject to any import fees or tariffs. Whether it's a $20 million Van Gogh painted in 1889 or a $2,000 sterling tea set stamped 1780, the item can come into the United States duty- and tax-free. Of course, you had better be an expert on the marketplace, because it would defeat the purpose to pay $50,000 for a painting in France and try to sell it in the U.S. and find it won't bring more than $20,000.

Whether you're dealing with "bad money" or "good money," banking is a conservative investment because once that money is banked it will only generate the 7- to 8-percent interest that certificates of deposit from stable countries yield. If you are looking for a higher rate of return and are willing to work to get it, there are other investment opportunities for "bad money" that you can take advantage of without taking your money out of the country. These opportunities can only start out as small-time ventures, but if you think in terms of a five-year plan, they have a chance to grow into sizable businesses that can absorb large amounts of cash safely.

This concept involves buying something that has little value, paying cash to greatly raise the value of the item, then selling the item for a large profit, on which you would pay taxes, or keeping it and borrowing it against its increased value.

The best example of this type of use for "bad money" is real estate. A booming marijuana-smuggling operation headquartered in Boston went by the *nom de guerre* of the "Boston Boys." As their cash reserves advanced to a point where they had a surplus with which to finance their next missions, they would buy run-down, decaying brownstones in the waterfront area of Boston. These buildings could be bought for very little money.

The Boston Boys would find workers willing to work for cash who would completely renovate the buildings. All supplies would be bought with cash, and the bulk of the money spent to fix up the property wouldn't show anywhere on paper. At this point the Boston Boys could sell the property at its increased value and then claim a taxable profit for themselves, or they could get the property appraised for its increased value and take the appraisal to a bank and borrow against it. That gave them legitimate borrowed funds with which to buy more properties to dump more "bad money" into.

Any item that presents an opportunity to buy it cheaply, invest cash in it to increase its value, and then sell it for the increased value is a possibility for laundering "bad money." This could include not only real estate but aircraft, cars, boats, fine watches, and antiques. A small business venture like this would provide you with the appearance of having a legitimate job, and it would not only allow you to launder some "bad money" but also give you the means to claim some income that you could pay taxes on.

For the student of money laundering, there is now a monthly, Miami-based publication, *Money Laundering Alert,* which is intended to acquaint the banking industry with the latest techniques in money laundering. It is not meant to inform the "bad guys," but it is nevertheless an accurate barometer of the latest money-laundering schemes. You'd probably find it interesting.

PART III

THE SMUGGLER AND THE JUSTICE SYSTEM

Two sets of laws have to be understood when dealing with drug crimes and the potential penalties: state laws and federal laws.

There are laws against crimes involving illegal drugs in all fifty states as well as in the federal code of laws. Thus, both the state and

CHAPTER 16

HE LAWS

the federal government could prosecute the same case. This means that if you are arrested in Chicago with five hundred pounds of marijuana in the trunk of your car, you can be prosecuted by the state of Illinois in state court and by the U.S. government in federal court. However, to be prosecuted by both federal and state courts is very rare and usually only happens in high-profile cases where federal prosecutors feel there has been a "failure of justice" in the state's effort.

Whereas it is rare for a single case to be prosecuted by both federal and state prosecutors, it is not that uncommon for federal prosecutors to come into a state and take over a drug case. There is no set rule as to why the feds will get involved in a case that would usually be handled by the state, but two main areas are important—money and publicity. The federal government has committed upwards of $11 billion to the war against drugs for fiscal year 1992, and you can bet that the politicians from President Bush on down are applying pressure to the various agencies that will receive this money to produce some spectacular results.

In October 1989, the manager of a warehouse complex in greater Los Angeles became suspicious of the activities of the three Hispanic men who rented one of his largest warehouses, where they claimed to be operating an import-export business.

The manager called the sheriff's department, which came to investigate. Inside they found twenty thousand pounds of cocaine, the largest seizure in the history of the United States.

No way would the feds let this grand cache of cocaine be attributed solely to the sheriff's department of some perimeter urban sprawl of Los Angeles. They rushed in and took this case away from the state of California in the interest of the publicity they could generate. Every time a news item appeared regarding this case, mention would be made of the largest seizure of cocaine ever in the United States, and words such as U.S. court, federal prosecutors, and DEA would appear. Anyone seeing these articles would assume that part of the great federal "drug" army had cracked this case and think that the $11 billion in federal tax dollars had been well-spent.

Often a state will invite federal prosecutors to handle a drug case if there is a high probability of developing a criminal conspiracy case on a national level. The feds are always happy to provide the money and manpower that the states lack to develop such a case against suspected drug felons.

In contrast to states' acceptance of federal assistance regarding drug prosecutions, the feds will rarely give a case its agencies have developed back to the states for trial. If the various federal agencies that are involved in the war on drugs have developed a case with their manpower and equipment, then the case will be handled by a federal prosecutor. It all has to do with publicity — how many arrests made, how many tons seized. That's important to the agencies and the politicians who vote for funding.

Some trends have become evident since the middle 1980s. States have to have balanced budgets by law; they can't run huge budget deficits like the federal government can. Since most states are overwhelmed with clogged court systems and vastly overcrowded prisons, the trend has been to happily accept federal assistance in prosecuting; then the convicted person goes into the federal prison system, not the state's.

Even with the $44-billion-and-climbing local, state, and national price tag on the war on drugs, funding it is still worth it to most elected politicians, as long as they can show statistics indicating that progress is being made in keeping drugs away from our school children.

A more recent development that has come with the almost yearly changes in the federal drug laws since 1984 has been for the feds to take cases away from the state in order to lengthen sentences. In the 1980s it became fashionable for politicians to campaign for tougher sentences and harsher laws against drug offenders, and the laws began to change.

With the 1984 Federal Crime Act, the federal government mandated longer sentences for drug offenders, and there has been a new federal drug act almost every year since 1984, further increasing sentences and mandatory minimum jail time. It should be noted that this mandatory minimum concept in the federal code of laws applies only to crimes involving drugs or weapons.

Today, the laws are so diverse and confusing that it is imperative that you know federal as well as state laws concerning the crime contemplated. The best way to get the latest information regarding laws and penalties is to make an appointment with a criminal attorney in the state you are operating in and have him or her explain the laws that could apply to you. A criminal attorney will know where to find the information and will be able to tell you, in plain English, what the laws and penalties are.

An attorney will charge from $100 to $150 an hour, which should be long enough for you to get the facts. You aren't going in there to say that you plan on flying a planeload of cocaine into the Orange County Airport on October 3 at 10 P.M. What you need to know are the California and federal laws and penalties involved with flying in thirty pounds of cocaine. A lawyer will give you an answer, and then you're aware of what's involved if you get caught.

A lot of people in the drug game don't even want to hear the words "laws and penalties." But the drug-smuggling game is a risk—freedom against financial reward—and the amount of freedom you are risking is something you should take into account when deciding if the risk is worth the payoff.

Besides having an idea of what potential penalties you would face if you got caught in your smuggling operation, there is one other good reason to be aware of the federal and state laws. The law that you might break probably has different parts to it; therefore, there are different degrees of punishment.

For example, on the federal level, possession of between 220 and 2,200 pounds of marijuana gets you at least five years with no parole and only fifty-four days a year (after the first year) of "good time" allowance (a reduction of a prisoner's sentence earned by cooperation and good behavior). Possession of 2,200 pounds or more marijuana gets you at least a ten-year federal mandatory minimum sentence without the possibility of parole and the same fifty-four days a year of good time. Armed with this information, you might decide to load your cigarette speedboat with only 2,100 pounds of marijuana instead of the 2,500 pounds you were planning on importing.

The strong arm of the law now goes beyond the person who is actually in possession of drugs or is involved in a conspiracy concerning drugs. Money laundering has joined the ranks of offenses that can result in long sentences. If federal prosecutors can prove that drug money was being laundered, they have a formula they use to convert the amount of money to pounds of cocaine or marijuana. The sentence is based on the amount of drugs computed to generate that much money.

The appendix in the back of this book has up-to-date information on the state and federal laws. As you can see, some states have much stricter laws than others. This is another factor that you should consider when planning where to conduct operations.

Don't be lazy. Every person involved in the effort should know the laws involved.

One evening the members of my smuggling group were sitting around talking about how many more missions we would attempt before we retired. We were discussing how much money we needed to live happily for the rest of our lives. "As long as things are going good, we'll never retire," someone said.

CHAPTER 17

UNTIL WE GET CAUGHT

"So you think we're going to keep doing this forever?" I asked.

"No, just till we get caught" was the reply.

Very few people retire from the smuggling business without experiencing a close or direct encounter with the U.S. judicial system in one form or another. This is a sobering statistic: of the twelve players who have been in the three groups I've worked with, ten have been arrested, nine have served jail time, and only two have made it through the battles with no dings on their records.

If this is indicative of what awaits a person in the smuggling business, you'd better pay attention.

In areas such as bail, search and seizure, and plea bargaining, there have been drastic changes, none of them beneficial to the smuggler who is unlucky enough to get caught. Smuggling laws are now changing almost yearly. Not only have the sentences been getting stiffer, but the basic framework of the law has changed as well.

Dealing with the legal system is something most smuggling groups don't contemplate until after the arrest of a group member or members. However, by having a preliminary knowledge of how the legal system—and the lawyers who inhabit it—conduct business, the members of a smuggling group can avoid a number of shocking realities once an arrest occurs. The following are some of the things that should be given careful consideration:

▶ *Be represented by a lawyer who is a criminal specialist with a high percentage of cases involving drugs.* Criminal lawyers stay abreast of the changes and trends in the law; they interact with other criminal lawyers, judges, clerks, and prosecutors on a daily basis.

▶ *Determine legal responsibility at the outset.* Everyone who is in jeopardy should know whether he will be taken care of by a lawyer retained by the group or if it will be his responsibility to find and pay for an attorney. Once anyone in a group is caught, the group needs to focus immediately on helping that person. Anxiety in a jailed person most often leads to everyone in the group being in legal jeopardy.

▶ *Have a working relationship with a criminal defense attorney.* A thousand-dollar retainer paid to an attorney will ensure his response to any problem you might encounter.

▶ *Lawyers' fees are open for bargaining.* There is no area of criminal law as lucrative as drug cases, since drug people generally have money. That's the perception among attorneys. A good criminal lawyer with ten years of experience can look at the particulars of a case and know instantly how much time will be involved to handle the motions, depositions, and trial, if it comes to that. Remember, no criminal attorney wants to pass up a drug case. Not only do drug defendants pay their bills, but an attorney knows that the initial drug case will lead to many more from the same group. A lawyer will appear in court for a bail hearing, file motions with the judge to attain the facts of the case, take depositions from witnesses, handle the plea bargain, and, as a last resort, represent the defense during a trial. For an average felony drug case that goes to trial, an attorney is looking at spending in the area of two weeks working directly on that case.

▶ *Unless you are caught in the same area in which your lawyer practices, your lawyer is going to have to hire a local attorney, who will do most of the work, and whom you must pay.*

▶ *If you have no money or don't want to spend what you have on an attorney, you will be assigned a public defender.* This doesn't necessarily mean you are going to get a longer sentence than if you had a private attorney. Conversely, having a public defender sometimes means you'll get a shorter sentence—the prosecutor sees no great challenge in doing battle with a public defender, because the client of a public defender is more than likely one of life's losers.

▶ *Never talk to anyone in law enforcement without your attorney being present.* Law enforcers are not your friends, they never will be your friends, and you aren't going to charm them out of anything. Beware of their common tendency to want to talk and make friends, even as they are leading you to jail.

A man is innocent until proven guilty. However, the law has now evolved to the point that if you're arrested for a federal crime involving drugs, the assumption is that you're probably guilty. Thus, so the logic goes, there is no sense in letting you out of jail before sentencing, since there is a strong possibility that you'll flee or, worse yet, commit more crimes while out on bond.

▶ *In drug-smuggling cases it is very possible that no bond will be issued.* You can't get out of jail unless the charges are dropped or you're proven innocent at a trial. No bond for drug crimes is a policy that is much more prevalent in the federal system. About the only way you'll get a bail bond with a federal drug charge is if you have a clean record and the case involves a mid-level to small-time operation that generates little or no publicity.

▶ *Bail bonds at the state level are set high for drug defendants initially—over $100,000.* Don't panic. These numbers aren't always what they seem. Bond terminology can run from a $100,000 full-cash bond to a $100,000 personal recognizance bond, meaning you only owe it if you don't show up when you're required to.

▶ *Use a bail bondsman.* You don't want to tie up your own money for what can be a period of three months to two years, and you don't want to have to explain to the court how it is that you possess a large sum of money when you have no job and have filed no income tax for the past five years.

If you are given no bond or an extremely high bond, you have the right to a bond-reduction hearing. If you are in a federal no-bond situation, you are entitled to a retention hearing. The American system of justice provides that a bail bond should not be punitive.

▶ *Most state and the federal court systems have a speedy-trial rule where criminal cases are concerned.* The time frame specified for a "speedy trial" is ninety days from arrest to trial. However, no matter when the trial takes place there will always be pretrial plea bargaining wherein the prosecutor will offer to reduce the charges or cap a sentence if the defendant will plead guilty, thus avoiding the expense of a trial.

▶ *A criminal case is not necessarily over when the judge pronounces sentence. The appeal process still remains.* An appeal of a verdict or sentence cannot be based on the facts of the case, but only on procedural errors that might have occurred. In just about every case that a criminal attorney loses, the standard line is that he will appeal; however, less than 5 to 7 percent of cases appealed in any given year are reversed.

▶ *If you choose to appeal a conviction, you have to negotiate another fee with your lawyer.* Five thousand dollars is a fair price to pay for an appeal of a case that went to trial, where the trial lasted three days or less. If the case did not go to trial and the appeal involves questioning the judge's decision on some motions or procedural points, then the fee should be in the area of $3,000 or less.

▶ *People involved in drug smuggling should realize that if they are caught, the best way for them to avoid preposterous sen-*

tences is to cooperate with the prosecution. It is stated in the federal criminal code that significant assistance by a defendant can result in less-than-minimum sentences being imposed. A prosecutor knows that there is always someone higher up than the defendant who is running the risk of getting caught—a "kingpin." This term means headlines, property seizures, promotions, and glory. If the prosecutor thinks a defendant has information that could result in a "kingpin" indictment, he is going to offer a deal to get it.

▶ *When faced with a jail sentence of more than a couple of years, a defendant is going to roll over and try to save himself if given the opportunity.* Forget about all the macho talk about how he would never cooperate with the cops. Once a defendant is offered the opportunity to cooperate with law enforcement, it is up to the defense attorney to spell out the agreement so the defendant doesn't unwittingly tell a story that will result in his being prosecuted for criminal activity that law enforcement wasn't aware of. This is generally accomplished by issuing a defendant blanket immunity from prosecution for all crimes he may have committed previously.

▶ *A person who has "flipped" will sometimes be required to provide information to a grand jury.* Being called before a grand jury means that your testimony is being requested in a more formal surrounding and that law enforcement is looking for information that will allow them to go for an indictment of another individual. It is also possible for anyone to be subpoenaed to appear before a grand jury if a prosecutor feels that this person might have information that will help him put the puzzle together. A summons to a grand jury offers options. If a person is a "cooperating" witness (who is giving testimony to save his own ass), then he's going to have to tell the truth—not volunteer information, just answer the questions.

A person can request immunity from prosecution for his testimony. If this is granted, nothing he says can be used against him. However, this does not mean that a case can't be developed against a person who has been granted limited immunity from the grand jury if outside sources are found. Ask Oliver North how this works.

A person can refuse to appear before a grand jury by fighting his subpoena. This tactic usually fails, and the result is that the person walks into the grand jury room and takes the Fifth Amendment, saying that he refuses to testify because he doesn't want to incriminate himself. Watch out for contempt of court on this one.

A person who has to face a grand jury who is not cooperating as a "flipped" witness, who doesn't want immunity, and who doesn't want to plead the Fifth, can try to duck the process by answering only the harmless questions truthfully and giving untruthful answers to questions that could harm other conspirators. There is no moral rule of behavior that says a person has to start telling the truth when he goes before a grand jury. However, the federal and state courts do not look favorably on this tactic should it be discovered.

▶ *When you enter the grand jury room to testify, your attorney cannot come with you.* However, your attorney can stay right outside the door, and if you are asked a question that you aren't comfortable answering spontaneously, you can stop the action and go outside to confer.

▶ *An investigation is required at the federal level and by most states prior to sentencing.* The presentence investigation is conducted to collect facts and background, which are put into a report form by the probation department, along with a recommendation of sentence for the judge to read and reflect on before pronouncing sentence.

It is possible for a defendant to hire people to prepare an extensive amendment to the presentence investigation, including an analysis of the average sentence for the specific crime, reports stating what a wonderful person the defendant is, letters with job offers in the event that the defendant should be granted probation, a private urinalysis to show the defendant is drug-free, and letters from social workers describing what a tremendous hardship the immediate family will endure if a defendant is jailed.

The federal system now has sentencing guidelines, and

except for very rare and extraordinary instances, a federal judge must sentence a defendant within the guidelines for the crime he has pleaded guilty to. Many states have adopted this method, and this has drastically reduced the leeway a judge has in sentencing a defendant.

Before the mid-1980s, most crimes involving drugs would carry a sentence that read something like "zero to twenty years." This has changed since the late 1980s. Mandatory sentences are now in effect at the federal level and for many states

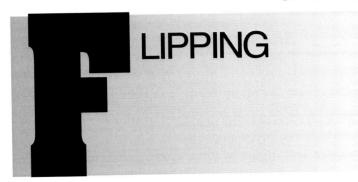

CHAPTER 18

FLIPPING

for all but personal possession of very small quantities of illegal drugs. With mandatory sentences, a judge no longer has many options as to the sentence he can give a convicted defendant. You can still hope to beat the case at trial; however, you can no longer hope for a lenient sentence. The main benefactor of this change is, of course, the prosecutor. The direct linkage of charges to sentences greatly increases his power over the plea-bargaining process.

Not all states have followed the federal government's lead regarding mandatory sentences. However, most of the states that have high levels of smuggling activity do have mandatory sentences, and you should know what they are before you commit the crime. Generally, the federal crimes carry the highest mandatory sentences, which, accentuated by the fact that there is no more parole in the federal system, means that a marijuana smuggler sentenced in a federal court might do as much jail time as someone convicted of murder in the state of Florida.

The hardest part of plea bargaining is psychological—dealing with the idea that you are going to have to plead guilty and then go to jail. A part of you keeps thinking that you aren't really guilty if your lawyer can win the case. The longer a case goes on, the more a defendant can convince himself that he is going to win. This leads to a defendant thinking that he can call the shots on his own case better than his attorney. That never works.

A person should go to trial when he is innocent, when there is a good chance his constitutional rights were violated, or when there is a probability that the prosecutor will not be able to convince the jury beyond a reasonable doubt. If any one of these three conditions don't exist, then look for a plea bargain.

Cooperating with law enforcement is the polite way of describing "flipping," "snitching," or being a "stool pigeon." However you want to refer to it, it's an option that an active drug smuggler should have in the back of his mind so he can be in a position to save himself a lot of extra jail time if he gets caught.

If your group is turned in, chances are an informant was convinced to "cooperate" with the DEA/FBI. Informants are usually people who have been busted before and have made a deal—leniency in return for information—or people who have been convinced by the DEA to provide information in exchange for money.

For example, when I was a part owner of an aircraft company in Boulder, Colorado, we rented, chartered, and sold aircraft to the general public. Every six months a DEA man would stop by to question me about who had rented our planes or purchased new ones and whether I thought any of them were suspicious and might be involved in drug smuggling. The carrot this DEA man held out was the immediate return of our plane should a pilot of one of our rental aircraft ever be busted for illegal activity. If I didn't cooperate, then who knew how long the paperwork could take before we would get the plane back—or if we would ever get it back.

In such situations, most people approached by the DEA/FBI will cooperate, and theirs could be the lead that gets a big conspiracy case started.

The year 1991 began with the United States finally reaching a goal that the politicians seemingly have been aiming for since the mid-1980s, when sentences for criminal activity, especially drug crimes, were greatly increased. The United States now incarcer-

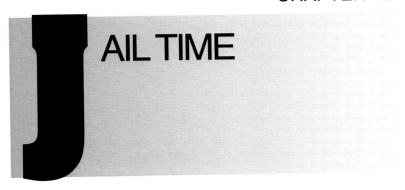

CHAPTER 19

JAIL TIME

ates a higher percentage of its population than any other country on Earth. We now have one out of every 250 people in the country behind county, state, or federal prison bars—or on parole or probation. Of this one million Americans under the direct supervision of the county, state, or federal divisions of corrections, roughly 40 to 50 percent are there for drug crimes of one kind or another. A player in the drug-smuggling battles had better think long and hard about how he might react if a judge tells him that he's going to prison.

In the United States the term "prison" encompasses three distinct correctional systems: county jails, state prisons, and federal institutions. Which system you might have to deal with almost always depends on just two things—which court system you are sentenced under, state or federal, and how long your sentence is.

County Jails
Every county in every state in America has a jail. The county jail serves three basic functions: to hold people who have been denied bond as they await federal or state trials, to hold people who have been sentenced as they await shipment to either state or federal prison, and to provide a place for people sentenced to

less than a year by a state court or less than three months by a federal court.

People may be in the county jail for anything from nonpayment of child support to murder. For this reason, county jails are very restrictive facilities where everyone is usually in locked cells and there are few recreational opportunities.

There may be four men in a cell designed for two, or sixty people in a dormitory designed for thirty. Exercise opportunities are limited, telephone access hard to come by, visiting periods short and controlled, and medical attention difficult to get if you have a medical problem. Most of your time is spent lying in a bunk contemplating just how you ended up in this situation while surrounded by some of the most ignorant, filthy, inconsiderate, and simpleminded human beings on Earth. Between sentencing and transport to a state or federal prison, time spent in county jail rarely lasts more than two months.

State Prisons

A state's prison system consists of many different prisons, ranging from maximum security to work camps with no fences. Where a person goes to serve his state time is determined by his age, length of sentence, type of crime, and past record.

Most maximum-security prisons involve living in cells or locked rooms. Medium- and minimum-security facilities mean dormitory living. Prisoners do the labor. The more skilled your background, the more skilled the job you will be assigned.

Most state prisons have libraries, telephone access, all-day visiting, TVs, gyms, outdoor recreational facilities, canteens, hobby shops, and educational courses from GED all the way up to college level.

In the last year of a state prison sentence, you can expect to go to a work-release facility. All states have such places, and they allow a person to work at a job in the private sector while living at the facility. In return for board, you give a percentage of your pay back to the state. Inmates are almost always placed in work-release facilities that are as close to family as possible. Some states also have policies where a work-release inmate who committed a nonviolent crime can receive furloughs.

Federal Prisons

Federal prison facilities and living conditions are vastly superior to state prison systems. By law, all fifty states are required to have balanced budgets, while we all know what the federal government thinks about deficit spending. Thus, federal prisons receive more funding than their state counterparts. This means better maintenance, a quicker response to overcrowding, and more programs for inmates. The federal system does not deal with the armed robbers, rapists, murderers, thieves, and street-level drug dealers that the state systems do; this means a more educated, older, and less volatile prison population.

Most federal prisoners with sentences under twelve years and no record of violence or use of weapons will find themselves assigned to a federal prison camp. If there is a record of weapons being used, then the prisoner will begin his federal time in a facility with a much more restrictive environment, not unlike what the states have to offer.

A federal prison camp is by far the best address. Federal prison camps are scattered around the United States, with most of them being located in close proximity to a "big house" or federal facility that houses medium- and high-security inmates.

Federal prison camps offer a small-college atmosphere. (Of course, the environment is male only, except for a few female guards.) Inmates go to their jobs, take classes, have recreation and meals, and watch TV with very little supervision. As long as an inmate is where he is supposed to be for the counts that take place every day, he can move about the grounds and buildings pretty much at will.

Once a federal camper passes a few drug tests and demonstrates to the administrators that he isn't going to be a problem, then he might have the opportunity to take college courses at a nearby university or be approved for up to five-day furloughs depending on the length of time he has left to serve.

Federal prison camps get media attention from time to time for being "country club" prisons, especially when high-profile personalities like Ivan Boesky, Michael Milken, or Pete Rose check in. The reality is that everyone works at an assigned job and has to follow strict rules. Campers may be in charge of maintenance at the golf course on a nearby air force base, but that task does not include a tee time for Sunday morning.

How Long?

From the moment a person enters prison, his number-one thought is, "When can I leave and get back to my life?" Unless someone is serving life without the possibility of parole, he will be getting out of prison way before he finishes his sentence.

Statutes and laws govern how state and federal institutions can reduce sentences. Thus, a person can have a very accurate idea of exactly how much time he will actually spend in custody.

The two main methods of sentence reduction are parole and good-time allowances.

Let's look at parole first. One of the offshoots of the Federal Sentencing Guidelines Act of 1988 was the elimination of parole for federal prisoners. Parole is no longer a possibility for people who committed a crime after the sentencing guideline act went into effect. However, parole still exists in most of the fifty states, and it is the way most state prisoners are released from prison.

State parole is not as arbitrary as it used to be before the huge prison population explosion of the 1980s. Most states now have a set of parole guidelines that are set forth by the state legislatures. These guidelines take into account the age of the inmate, his marital status, educational level, previous convictions, previous jail time, and whether or not violence was involved. A score is formulated, and then that score is factored into a matrix to come up with how much time an inmate has to complete.

I received a five-year sentence for my crime of possession of more than five grams of marijuana. To compute my "salient" score, Florida considered my age (thirties), previous arrest record (none), previous jail record (none), whether a gun was used in my crime (no), and my educational level (college grad). My salient score was zero, and this was compared on a graph to the crime I had committed. The graph showed I should be paroled at between eleven and fifteen months. Thus, I only served fifteen months of my five-year sentence.

The state parole guidelines work out well for everyone. A judge can give a preposterous sentence and keep his hardass reputation intact, while a state can then parole the person and avoid paying the huge cost of incarceration. Also, truly violent and dangerous criminals are kept locked up, while nonviolent, mostly drug criminals don't have to serve the draconian sentences some judges feel compelled to give.

The second method by which state and federal sentences are reduced is by good time. Good time was originally set up as a reward to inmates for not being troublemakers. However, since the prison population explosion of the 1980s, good-time rewards are now programs that can be quickly modified to avert prison overcrowding at the state level.

However, at the federal level, the Sentencing Guidelines Act of 1988 drastically reduced good-time allowances for federal inmates. Presently, a federal inmate only receives fifty-four days of good time a year, and that doesn't start until the second year of the sentence. This is in contrast to federal good-time allowances prior to 1988 that awarded up to 120 days a year of sentence relief, or the state of Texas, which awards ten days of good time for every day served.

Good-time allowances have the backing of law, and unless someone attacks a guard or gets caught escaping, it is rare for those allowances to be taken away.

There is a viable option to going to jail. That is to become a fugitive from justice.

When I was serving time in the state of Florida, my prison job was to assist a famous prisoner, Judge Joe Peel, in the law library.

CHAPTER 20

THE FUGITIVE

Joe Peel was a convicted double murderer serving life, but as part of an American Civil Liberties Union (ACLU) case, Joe was set up in an office to provide legal aid to inmates. My job was to screen the inmates who wanted Joe's help.

As a result of this job, I heard hundreds of stories every week from inmates who were looking to appeal verdicts, get sentence reductions, file parole appeals, and generally come up with a host of other legal maneuvers. I was amazed when people were allowed to stay out on bond to get affairs in order after being sentenced to twenty-five years by the judge and would then turn themselves in. "Why did you do it," I'd ask, "when you knew you have to do eight or nine years before parole? Why not get a new set of IDs and start a new life?"

Most inmates had no answer for my question besides saying that they had been caught committing a crime and wanted to pay their debt to society. I was appalled—since when is a person worried about paying a debt to a society whose laws he knowingly violated in the first place? Joe Peel had the real answer to why people would show up to begin their sentences and not run away. Joe's theory was that most prisoners enter prison broke and realize that the only way they can make a living is by continuing their criminal activities. With no money and no marketable skills, that leaves just one's family, and if a person chose to become a fugitive, he would have to cut himself off from the few people who might care about him—or risk implicating them on an aiding-and-abetting-a-fugitive charge. For most people, this loss of family contact was too much; they'd rather do the prison time.

But the drug and drug-smuggling professions have added a new wrinkle to Judge Joe Peel's theory. Many people in the drug business have accumulated a substantial degree of wealth by the time they are caught, plus they have the skills and contacts that offer the possibility of large payoffs if they keep working. To these people, the fugitive option is a real possibility.

If you do choose to go this route, it is helpful to know that law enforcement probably will make little or no effort to get you back. If a person escapes prison, law enforcement might search the local grounds and check the bus station, but nothing that would keep them away from the coffee pot for very long. If the situation involves a person who is not making a court appearance—or not showing up to begin serving a sentence—then the effort isn't going to be much more than a telephone call to that person's house.

The individual most concerned when a person becomes a fugitive is his bondsman. That's money out of his pocket. It is a good idea to pay off your bondsman in full before jumping ship, because this eliminates the one person who is going to make the biggest effort to locate you.

There are two reasons law enforcement doesn't go running after drug-smuggler fugitives. First, they don't have the money or manpower to do the street-pounding detective work necessary to find people who go underground. The other reason is that they know most fugitives will apprehend themselves within six months. The name goes in the various criminal computer banks, and then they wait for results. You get stopped for a traffic violation, and the cops run the driver's license; you're coming back from a vacation in the Bahamas, and customs runs your name through the entry computers. When the bells start ringing, law enforcement detains you and figures out why you're wanted.

Law enforcement also knows, from statistics, that most fugitives will continue their life of crime and thus will get caught again.

However, the drug business has changed the stereotype of a fugitive. People in the drug business really do post million-dollar bonds and then bolt, and they often do have the resources to try and bribe low-paid court workers to make an honest mistake that will get them removed from criminal computers.

A successful fugitive in the 1990s will, above all, need money so he can avoid having to keep committing crimes to provide for himself and his family. He will also need an impeccable set of identification for himself and his wife, plus an ego that will allow him to sever contact with all but a few trusted family members and friends.

The final fact a fugitive has to face is that he must leave the United States. Staying in the United States poses too many opportunities for a slip-up that could result in capture.

When I was doing prison time in the state of Florida, I'd often sit in the law library and read monthly case-law books, checking the current editions for the latest drug-related search-and-seizure cases. I'd read about how a man had shown up at the ticket counter

PILOGUE

at Miami International dressed in a fur coat with visible white residue around his nostrils, and the appellate court had confirmed the lower-court ruling that the airport cops had probable cause in stopping the man to ask him some questions. I'd lean back in my chair and smugly think that I'd never do anything as stupid as that.

Then one day in 1979, the monthly Florida case-law book arrived at the prison law library, and this book contained the brief on the appeal of the case that had sent me to prison. I asked Judge Joe Peel, the famous prisoner who ran the law library, to read the case.

Joe read the four-page brief and started laughing as he put the book down on the desk. "Kenny, how could you be so stupid?" he asked. "You fly a plane into south Florida with the windows covered by tinfoil? That might be a good look for going to the moon, but south Florida? What were you thinking?"

What I was thinking at the time was that the tinfoil covering up the window did look horrible, but there really wasn't a good alternative when time and money were factored in. What I should have been thinking was that it was suicide to land a plane full of marijuana, for a refueling stop in south Florida. Especially an airplane that had all its windows covered from the inside with tinfoil.

Joe Peel deserved a good laugh at my smuggling group's stupidity, just as I would laugh at others whom I read about in case briefs that had done things equally as dumb as covering their smuggling plane's windows with tinfoil so no one could see inside. However, it's easy to laugh at a smuggling group's mistakes after the fact; it's a lot harder to correct a disaster before it happens.

In Hollywood, if someone makes a movie about a black cop and white cop who are a team (*Lethal Weapon*), and that movie goes on to gross $150 million at the box office, then within a year, Hollywood will have five movies released based on the same premise. With drug smuggling, if one group finds a successful penetration area for the contraband cargo to enter the United States, this information will never be revealed. Thus, in effect, every smuggling group is operating independently and with no cross-flow of information. The same mistakes are destined to happen over and over again.

I refer to drug smuggling runs as "missions" because there wasn't any difference between flying the missions I flew in Vietnam and flying drug trips to Jamaica or Colombia. They both involved planning, assignment of jobs to group members, followed by the adventure and danger of the trip itself. We learned by on-the-job training and desperately tried not to repeat mistakes, but you could never figure where the next potential disaster would come from.

If a smuggling group could have the benefit of hiring a moonlighting FBI/DEA agent, a radar technician, a man on the design team of the F-117A Stealth fighter, a U.S. Customs officer, an officer of a coast guard cutter stationed in south Florida, and the chief of police of the county where illegal operations are going to occur, the knowledge base of these people would definitely elevate the odds that the planned mission would succeed. However, smuggling groups don't get to hire talent like this to "consult" them.

Nevertheless, information exists that explains and speculates on how law enforcement is going to move next in order to foil the entrepreneurial drug smuggler of the 1990s. The intent of this book has been to build a foundation for a knowledge base that anyone involved in — or thinking of being involved in — drug smuggling should have. However, the information contained in this book is only a foundation; layers and layers of new, more current data exists, and the smuggling groups that can realize the importance of gathering and utilizing this incoming data to modify and improve their operations will be those that succeed in the 1990s.

I am not going to conclude this book by preaching that you should learn from my experience that drug smuggling will only lead to wasted years, jail time, and an unproductive life. On the contrary, all the major players in smuggling groups I have been associated with have made large amounts of money, enough to lessen the problem of the jail time they had to serve.

We've also lived our late twenties and thirties playing combat, but in a war that offers more than a pat on the back from a colonel who wears his hair in a crew cut.

I never felt good about the missions I flew in Vietnam when I was a warrior supposedly on the side of truth and the American way. However, my marijuana-smuggling trips were entirely different. I almost felt I was the Vietcong, once again challenging the flawed thinking of the seventy-year-old, conservative, multimillionaires who run the United States.

For me the decision to be involved in drug smuggling was one of diminishing options for an airline flying career after I left the air force. If an airline career wasn't possible, then I took the skills I had acquired and applied them somewhere that they were in demand.

I've often been asked how I would solve the supposed drug problem in the United States. People seem to expect me, as a convicted smuggler, to answer that I'd legalize all drugs, placing them in the same heavily taxed, over-twenty-one realm of tobacco and alcohol. This is not the case.

Legalization is the answer I would give *if I were somehow elected president of the United States*; however, my personal response is that I do not want to see anything done that would change the status of illegal drugs. It is a comforting thought to know that the opportunity exists for me to saddle up the ol' airplane and roll the dice for a million-dollar-plus payday if I so choose. That's the real American dream, and I would not like to see that possibility disappear.

On the chart that follows, the weights of 300 pounds of mari-juana, 3,000 pounds of marijuana, 5 pounds of cocaine, and 200 pounds of cocaine were chosen to demonstrate the difference in possible penalties between a load that could easily fit in the trunk

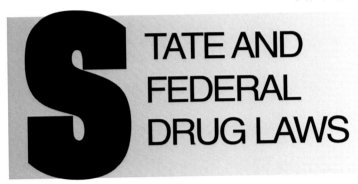

STATE AND FEDERAL DRUG LAWS

of your car and one that would require extensive contacts and organization to smuggle.

When sentences are imposed for drug crimes, often the terms, mandatory minimums, sentencing guidelines, and presumptive sentences will be used. This Appendix lists the lowest and the highest penalties possible for the specific type and weight of contraband. (Michigan had the toughest penalties until just before this book went to press, when the state Supreme Court ruled the laws unconstitutional on the grounds that they constituted "cruel *or* unusual" punishment. Prior to that, possession of more than 650 grams [1.4 pounds] of cocaine resulted in a mandatory life sentence with no possibility for parole in Michigan.) Situations such as whether a weapon was used in the commission of a felony and how many prior offenses an individual has on his record can mean that the listed sentences could be even more lengthy.

Also, in all of the state and the federal statutes, there is a second part to a sentence in addition to the length of time that must be served. This involves monetary fines, which, in many cases, can be in the millions of dollars. Suffice it to say that the government will either confiscate any money or assets that can be proven to have been attained through illegal activity—or force you to remunerate in the form of a monetary fine added to your sentence.

STATE	POSSESSION/SALE 300 LBS MARIJUANA	POSSESSION/SALE 3,000 LBS MARIJUANA	POSSESSION/SALE 5 LBS COCAINE
AL	5 YRS.–LIFE	LIFE W/O PAROLE	15 YRS.–LIFE
AK	0–5 YRS.	0–5 YRS.	0–10 YRS.
AZ	5–14 YRS.	5–14 YRS.	5–14 YRS.
AR	6–30 YRS.	6–30 YRS.	40 YRS.–LIFE
CA	2–4 YRS.	2–4 YRS.	2–15 YRS.
CO	2–8 YRS.	2–8 YRS.	4–16 YRS.
CT	5–20 YRS.	5–20 YRS.	5 YRS.–LIFE
DE	5 YRS.	15 YRS.	15 YRS.
FL	3–30 YRS.	5–30 YRS.	15–30 YRS.
GA	5 YRS.	7 YRS.	25 YRS.
HI	0–10 YRS.	0–10 YRS.	20 YRS.
ID	0–5 YRS.	0–5 YRS.	0 YRS.–LIFE
IL	3–7 YRS.	3–7 YRS	15–60 YRS.
IN	2–8 YRS.	2–8 YRS.	20–50 YRS.
IA	0–50 YRS.	0–50 YRS.	0–50 YRS.
KS	3–20 YRS.	3–20 YRS.	3–20 YRS.
KY	5–10 YRS.	5–10 YRS.	5–10 YRS.
LA	5–15 YRS.	10–40 YRS.	15–30 YRS.
ME	5–10 YRS.	5–10 YRS.	10 YRS.
MD	5 YRS.–LIFE	5 YRS.–LIFE	5 YRS.–LIFE
MA	3–15 YRS.	5–15 YRS.	15–20 YRS.
MI	0–4 YRS.	0–4 YRS.	LIFE
MN	0–30 YRS.	0–30 YRS.	0–30 YRS.
MS	1–30 YRS.	1–30 YRS.	1–30 YRS.
MO	10–30 YRS.	10–30 YRS.	10–30 YRS.
MT	1–5 YRS.	1–5 YRS.	2–20 YRS.

POSSESSION/SALE 200 LBS COCAINE	WILL RELEASE ON PAROLE	GOOD TIME ALLOWANCE PER/YR SERVED	LAWYER PROVIDING INFORMATION
LIFE W/O PAROLE	YES	VARIABLE	J. WILSON DINSMORE (205) 252-9751
0–10 YRS.	YES	120	THOMAS NAVE (907) 586-3309
5–14 YRS.	YES	VARIABLE	BRUCE FEDER (602) 257-0135
40 YRS.–LIFE	YES	360 DAYS	LITTLE ROCK DRUG TASK FORCE
2–15 YRS.	YES	360 DAYS	SAN FRANCISCO DA
4–16 YRS.	YES	360 DAYS	PATRICK MIKA (719) 473-1500
5 YRS.–LIFE	YES	UP TO 540 DAYS	CT STATE ATTY.
15 YRS.	NO	NOT FOR HIGH-WEIGHT SENTENCES	JOHN MALIK (302) 427-2247
15–30 YRS.	NO	120 DAYS	RUSS CRAWFORD (407) 425-8659
25 YRS.	YES	240 DAYS	TERRY JACKSON (912) 232-2646
20 YRS.	YES	NONE	HONOLULU PUBLIC DEFENDER
0 YRS.–LIFE	YES	NONE	ALAN TRIMMING (208) 343-6466
15–60 YRS.	NO	360 DAYS	GEORGE TASEFF (309) 827-5425
20–50 YRS.	YES	2 FOR 1	STEPHEN DILLON (317) 923-9391
0–50 YRS.	YES	182 DAYS	MARION BEATTY (319) 382-4226
3–20 YRS.	YES	360 DAYS	WITCHITA DA
5–10 YRS.	YES	30 DAYS	COMMONWEALTH ATTY'S OFFICE
15–30 YRS.	YES	2 FOR 1 (1st OFFENSE)	ROBERT GLASS (504) 581-9065
10 YRS.	NO	135 DAYS	RICHARD EMERSON (207) 773-0275
5 YRS.–LIFE	YES, AFTER MANDATORY MIN.	120 DAYS	MICHAEL KAMINKOW (302) 659-0111
15–20 YRS.	YES	120 DAYS	JOE OTERI (617) 227-3700
LIFE	YES	50 DAYS	DRUG CRIMES UNIT OFFICE
0–30 YRS.	YES	120 DAYS	MARK KURZMAN (612) 871-9004
1–30 YRS.	YES	270 DAYS	BILOXI SPECIAL CRIME UNIT
10–30 YRS.`	YES	240 DAYS	DONALD COOLEY (417) 883-8200
2–20 YRS.	YES	UP TO 360 DAYS	BILLINGS COUNTY ATTY.

STATE	POSSESSION/SALE 300 LBS MARIJUANA	POSSESSION/SALE 3,000 LBS MARIJUANA	POSSESSION/SALE 5 LBS COCAINE
NE	0–5 YRS.	0–5 YRS.	5–50 YRS.
NV	3–20 YRS.	5–20 YRS.	25 YRS.–LIFE
NH	10–20 YRS.	10–20 YRS.	15–30 YRS.
NJ	0–10 YRS.	0–10 YRS.	5–20 YRS.
NM	3 YRS.	3 YRS.	9 YRS.
NY	0–15 YRS.	0–15 YRS.	15 YRS.–LIFE
NC	7 YRS. MIN.	14 YRS. MIN.	35 YRS. MIN.
ND	0–20 YRS.	0–20 YRS.	0–20 YRS.
OH	2–15 YRS	2–15 YRS.	15 YRS.–LIFE
OK	4 YRS.–LIFE	4 YRS.–LIFE	10 YRS.–LIFE
OR	0–10 YRS.	0–10 YRS.	0–10 YRS.
PA	5 YRS.	5–10 YRS.	4–10 YRS.
RI	0–30 YRS.	0–30 YRS.	20 YRS.–LIFE
SC	25 YRS.	25 YRS.	25–30 YRS.
SD	0–10 YRS.	0–10 YRS.	0–10 YRS.
TN	15 YRS.–LIFE	15 YRS.–LIFE	15 YRS.–LIFE
TX	10 YRS.–LIFE	15–99 YRS.	15–99 YRS.
UT	0–5 YRS.	0–5 YRS.	1–15 YRS.
VT	0–15 YRS.	0–15 YRS.	0–20 YRS.
VA	5–30 YRS.	5–30 YRS.	5–40 YRS.
WA	0–5 YRS.	0–5 YRS.	0–10 YRS.
WV	1–5 YRS.	1–5 YRS	1–15 YRS.
WI	1–10 YRS.	1–10 YRS.	10–30 YRS.
WY	0–10 YRS.	0–10 YRS.	0–20 YRS.
FEDERAL	5–40 YRS.	10 YRS.–LIFE	5–40 YRS.

POSSESSION/SALE 200 LBS COCAINE	WILL RELEASE ON PAROLE	GOOD TIME ALLOWANCE PER/YR SERVED	LAWYER PROVIDING INFORMATION
5–50 YRS.	YES	120 DAYS	JAMES DAVIS (402) 341-9900
25 YRS.–LIFE	YES, AFTER MANDATORY MIN.	120 DAYS	MITCHELL POSIN (702) 382-5315
15–30 YRS.	YES	NONE	CATHY GREEN (603) 669-8446
5–20 YRS.	YES	130 DAYS	PVT. ATTY.— NAME WITHHELD
9 YRS.	YES	360 DAYS	MIKE ROSENBERG (505) 842-6742
15 YRS.–LIFE	YES	120 DAYS	BROOKLYN DA
35 YRS. MIN.	NO	182 DAYS	CHARLES MORGAN (704) 334-9669
0 YRS.–LIFE	YES	60 DAYS	ROBERT WEFALD (701) 258-8945
15 YRS. –LIFE	YES	100 DAYS	COLUMBUS DA
10 YRS.–LIFE	YES	VARIABLE	PAUL BURTON (918) 585-1600
0–10 YRS.	YES	70 DAYS	ROSS SHEPARD (503) 484-2611
4–10 YRS.	YES	NONE	DIANNE DICKSON (215) 437-4896
20 YRS.–LIFE	YES	70 DAYS/YR.	RICK CORLEY (401) 863-8800
25–30 YRS.	NO	VARIABLE	STUART FELDMAN (803) 722-7745
0–10 YRS.	YES	120 DAYS	SIOUX FALLS. STATE ATTY.
15 YRS.–LIFE	YES	720 DAYS	NASHVILLE DRUG TASK FORCE
15–99 YRS.	YES	UP TO 10 FOR 1	JEFF BLACKBURN (806) 371-8333
1–15 YRS.	YES	NONE	STEPHEN McCAUGHEY (801) 364-6474
0–20 YRS.	YES	120 DAYS	PVT. ATTY.— NAME WITHHELD
5–40 YRS.	YES	180 DAYS	JOHN ZWERLING (703) 684-7900
0–10 YRS.	NO	120 DAYS/YR.	JEFFREY STEINBORN (206) 622-5117
1–15 YRS.	YES	360 DAYS	CHARLESTON PROSECUTING ATTY.
10–30 YRS.	YES	NONE	DAVID MANDELL (608) 256-7765
0–20 YRS.	YES	120 DAYS	CHYENNE DA
10 YRS.–LIFE	NO	54 DAYS	RUSS CRAWFORD (407) 425-8659

The rules governing parole are far too numerous to be listed in this Appendix. In states that have parole, it is possible that you will have to serve a certain percentage of your sentence before you are eligible to go before the parole board. It is also possible that your appearance before a parole board will be controlled by parole guidelines enacted by the state legislature in the state where you are serving your time. With a mandatory minimum sentence, you will have to serve the mandatory part of the sentence before you are eligible for parole.

Good-time allowance usually allows you to earn different amounts of good time based on how long your sentence is, what kind of job you perform while in prison, and whether you attend self-help classes. The possibilities are too numerous to mention, but you can call the Bureau of Prisons of the state you are interested in for more specific information.

The attorneys listed, all of who specialize in the practice of criminal law and have vast experience in narcotics cases, provided the information included in this Appendix. In cases where I could not get the necessary information from a criminal attorney, I contacted the various district attorneys' offices or other state institutions.

Remember, when dealing with large amounts of marijuana or cocaine, it is more than likely that the federal government will take over a case from the state to ensure that a conviction will mean a lengthy period of actual prison time served.

K. Hawkeye Gross grew up on the North Shore of Chicago. He graduated from the University of Colorado in 1968, then enlisted in the U.S. Air Force, serving in Vietnam from 1970 to 1971 as a Forward Air Control (FAC) pilot in the 0-2 aircraft. He flew 330

ABOUT
THE AUTHOR

combat missions and earned the Air Medal as well as a Distinguished Flying Cross.

Mr. Gross has also logged many combat flights to Colombia and Jamaica in the ongoing marijuana wars. No medals have been issued for these missions.

He presently lives in the mountains of Colorado with his wife and 11-year-old son.